We're very big in racing.

Racing is in our blood. Racing is in our products. For over thirty years we've been engineering winning performance both on and off the track.

If you are looking to improve the performance of your car, look for the STP trademark. After all, who has a better track record?

FIRST BRANDS CORPORATION

Here's to Al Jr., Paul, Emmo, and their crews for a season full of victory.

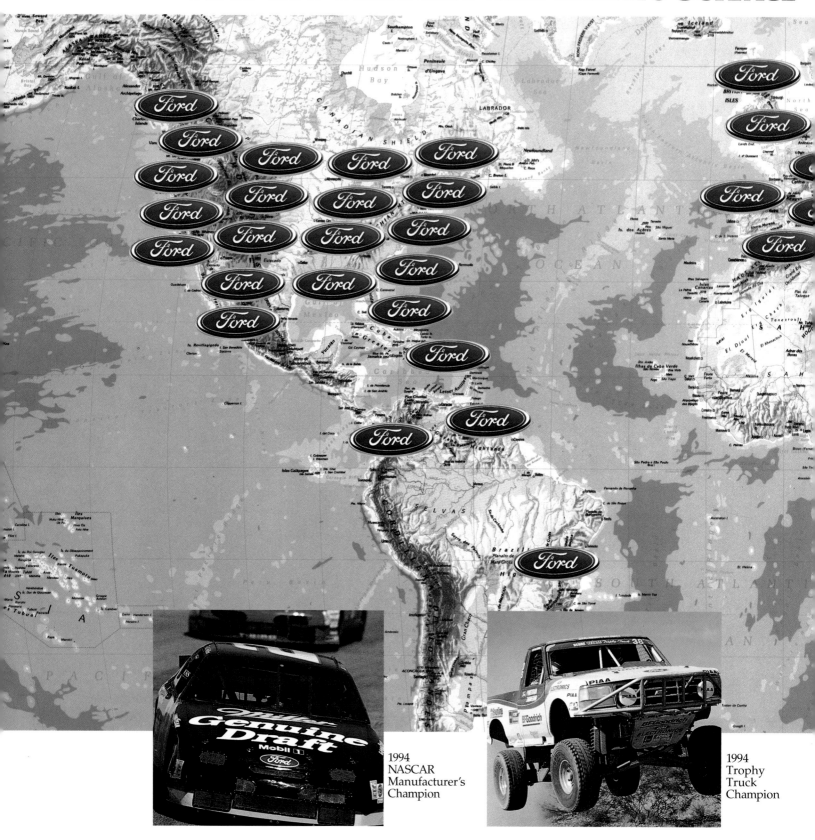

1994
NASCAR
Manufacturer's
Champion

1994
Trophy
Truck
Champion

There are oceans. And then there's something that's really big and blue. Once again, the Ford Oval has made its mark across the world. It's called racing success, and no other automaker can make a claim of such global proportions. But at Ford, no matter where on Earth we capture another checkered flag, we always bring home the most interesting

WAS DOMINATED BY WATER.

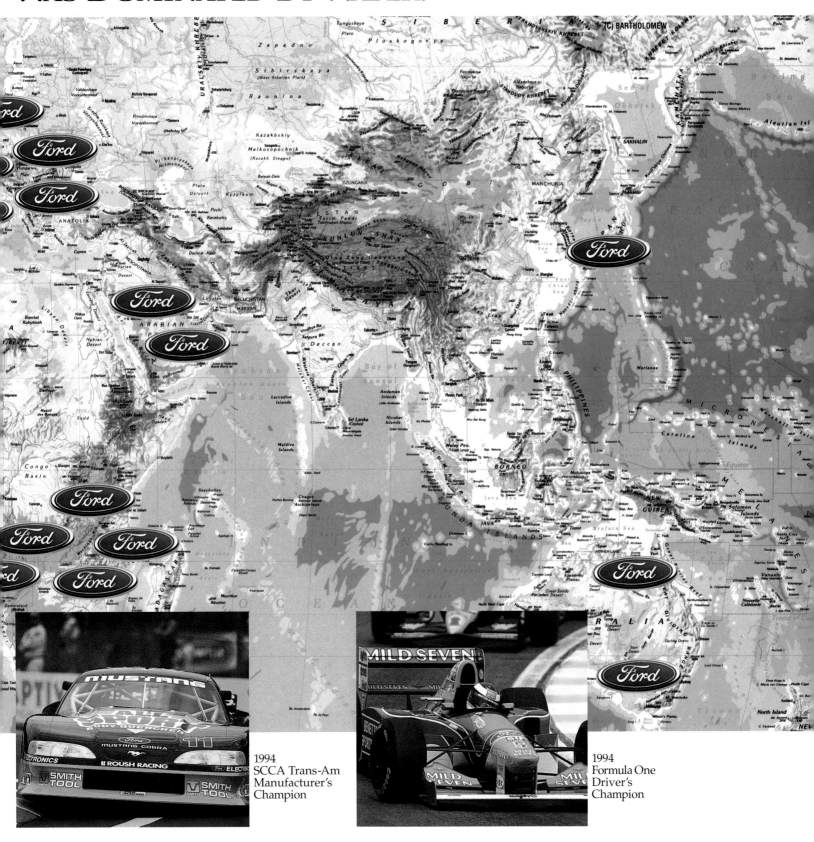

1994
SCCA Trans-Am
Manufacturer's
Champion

1994
Formula One
Driver's
Champion

souvenirs. One weekend, it may be an idea on steering components from a hairpin curve in Monaco. Another weekend, a lesson in durability from off-road shock treatments in the Baja desert. Of course, the end result is simple: More winning technology for the Ford car or truck you can drive. Looks like we have everything covered.

A PENSKE PINNACLE

A year to be remembered…Even Roger Penske will find it difficult to match his PPG Cup winning '94 IndyCar campaign. The stark statistics tell only part of the story. 12 victories for his Marlboro Team Penske in the 16 races contested, including the "big one", the Indianapolis 500. What the statistics don't tell is that the team's "in house" chassis and engines, its driving and engineering talent were all superb. Coupled with Penske generalship, they were insurmountable.

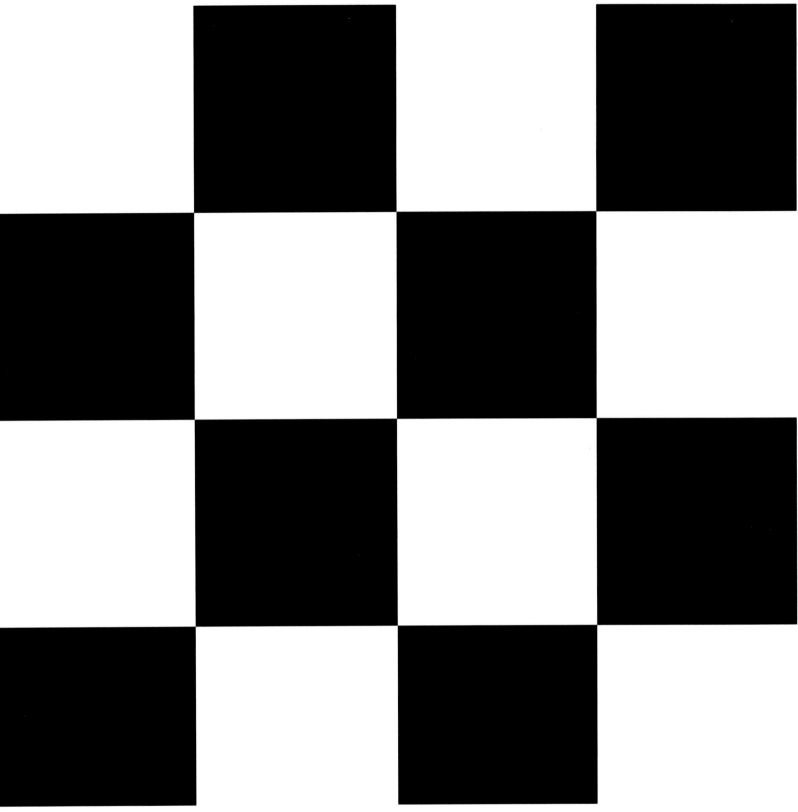

THIS YEAR ROGER PENSKE SHOWED THE WORLD HIS TRUE COLORS.

It was a banner year for racing team owner Roger Penske. Not only did his Marlboro Team Penske break the all-time record for the most wins in an Indy Car season, drivers Al Unser, Jr., Paul Tracy and Emerson Fittipaldi scored five 1-2-3 finishes, securing two new places in the record books.

Which is where Miller Team Penske is headed as Rusty

Wallace leads the NASCAR field with more wins in the last two years than any other driver.

And both teams did it with Mobil 1® synthetic motor oil, the very same Mobil 1 you can use in your car.

So congratulations, Roger, on a championship year. We'll remember it just like you saw it. In vivid black and white.

Keeps your engine running like new.

CONTENTS

Published by: Autosport International, Inc.
Publisher: John H. Norwood
Associate Publisher: Barbara Hassler-Steig
Design Director: Robert Steig
Editor: Jonathan Hughes

Front Cover Photography: Geoffrey Hewitt, Nigel Kinrade, Steve Mohlenkamp, David Taylor
Contributing Photographers: Cheryl Day Anderson, Dan Bianchi, Michael C. Brown, Daytona International Speedway, Geoffrey Hewitt, Indianapolis Motor Speedway, Nigel Kinrade, Brian Leshon, Brian A. Mitchell, Steve Mohlenkamp, Linda McQueeney, Ron McQueeney, Bob Steig, Steve Swope, David Taylor, Paul Webb, Eric Wunrow

Motorsports America, The Men & Machines of American Motorsport, 1994-95
is published by Autosport International, Inc.
344 East 51 Street, New York, NY 10022
© 1995 Autosport International, Inc.
No part may be reproduced without prior written permission.
Distributed in the U.S. by Motorbooks International, Osceola, WI 54020
Printed in the U.S.A.

"One thing you learn in racing is that they don't wait for you." *Roger Penske*

When he was fourteen years old, Roger Penske's father took him to see his first Indianapolis 500. "The crowd, the excitement—it just got to me," Penske recalls. "I said to myself, 'Someday I'm going to compete here.'"

Eighteen years later he made it to Indy as the leader of Team Penske. To date, they have won ten Indy 500 victories, and are the most successful team ever.

In addition to managing his racing team, Penske runs an international multi-billion-dollar transportation business. "I try to teach my people that it's up to them to innovate, to make things happen."

Roger Penske combines a focus on results with attention to detail. "What I like about Rolex," he explains, "is that they don't compromise either. That's why I've worn a Rolex for over two decades."

ROLEX

Rolex Oyster Perpetual Day-Date Chronometer in 18kt gold with matching concealed-clasp President bracelet.
Write for brochure. Rolex Watch U.S.A., Inc., Dept. 477, Rolex Building, 665 Fifth Avenue, New York, N.Y. 10022-5383.
Rolex, ♔, Oyster Perpetual, Day-Date and President are trademarks.

The 1995 Monte Carlo. Com

We've told you for years that no car company brings more race-winning technology to the street than Chevrolet. What we haven't told you is that some of our finest ideas to improve our racing program come from the street. Check out the 1995 Monte Carlo Z34. Designed to be your own personal space, the Monte Carlo Z34 features front seats that are deeply contoured. The

Sterling Marlin's Kodak Chevrolet which won last year's Daytona 500 is parked next to the Monte Carlo Z34 which makes its racing debut at this year's Daytona 500.

ng to a winner's circle near you.

instrument panel and controls are laid out just the way you said they should be. You'll get a fuel-injected V6, the safety of dual air bags and anti-lock brakes. It's already a winner on the street. And it's sure to keep our winning tradition alive on the track. After all, one car company has won more races in the history of NASCAR. Genuine Chevrolet.

MONTE CARLO

GENUINE CHEVROLET™

LeRoy Neiman and Mario Andretti

B Steig

DRIVER OF THE QUARTER CENTURY

Mario Andretti leaves the IndyCar arena after a career spanning 31 years. His 52 wins, 67 poles, 4 national championships, and the all-time lap leadership are testimonials to his brilliance and intensity. Distinguished artist LeRoy Neiman, an ardent motorsports disciple, captures some highpoints of Andretti's multifaceted life behind the wheel.

FROM WIPERS TO RAIN-X.

GREG PICKETT
1994 RAIN-X/CYTOMAX
CHEVROLET CAMARO

Unelko Corporation 7428 East Karen Drive Scottsdale, AZ 85260 (602) 991-7272 FAX (602) 483-7674

& NOW!

FAMILY SIZE

THE INVISIBLE WINDSHIELD WIPER®

rain·X®

Dramatically improves wet weather driving visibility–disperses rain, sleet & snow on contact–lets you see clearly–with and without wipers!

RAIN-X seals–polishes–protects glass & plastic windshields, side & rear windows, mirrors & lights with an invisible super-slick, non-stick coating. Makes water "bead" for aero-dynamic runoff. RAIN-X restricts bug, frost, salt, mud, oil, dust & road film adhesion–makes cleaning a snap–prevents parching from sun, sand and pollutants. Use RAIN-X for increased all-around visibility, safety and driving comfort.

CAUTION: FLAMMABLE–EYE IRRITANT – Read Back Label

16 FL. OZ. (473ml)

NEW!

rain·Rx®

OIL ENERGIZER
LUBRICITY MULTIPLIER

PRESCRIPTION FOR ALL INTERNAL COMBUSTION ENGINES

"MAKES EVEN THE BEST OIL BETTER!"

- Reduces Emissions
- Saves Gas
- Extends Oil Life
- Retards Engine Wear
- Increases Horsepower
- Improves Performance

A BREAKTHROUGH IN LUBRICATION

16 fl. oz (473 ml)

FAMILY SIZE

rain·X® anti-FOG

& GLASS CLEANER CONCENTRATE
FOR HOME AND AUTO
INTERIOR GLASS & MIRRORS

NEW TECHNOLOGY
INSTANT WIPE-ON FORMULA

CLEANS AND CONDITIONS

CAUTION: FLAMMABLE–EYE IRRITANT–read back label

16 FL. OZ. (473 ml)

Rx Oil Energizer™ provides the essential oil nutrients required to dramatically improve performance, retard wear and tear of internal parts, and reduce exhaust emissions…while at least doubling engine oil life to save money, extend recycling intervals and conserve vital resources.

Precision engineered to neutralize contaminants, prevent corrosion and reduce emissions. Compare your emissions test results before and after adding Rx Oil Energizer™.

As Featured On:

THE WEATHER CHANNEL®

Weather You Can Always Turn To™

THIS YEAR, THE SUPRA WILL HAVE ITS MOST IMPRESSIVE FOLLOWING EVER.

There are accolades from the press. "Oohs" and "aahs" from people on the street. But this year, the Toyota Supra Turbo will hear something really special in its wake. The roar of powerful engines. Because Supra Turbo is the "Official PPG Pace Car" of the three Toyota-sponsored Indy car events for 1995...Miami...Long Beach...Monterey. With its twin turbos, 320 hp and ability to go 0 to 60 mph in 4.6 seconds,* the Supra Turbo is a natural-born leader. Think about it. The hottest cars on the track paced by one of the hottest cars on the street. So tune in. Because not since the broadcast of a space shuttle launch has an afternoon of TV been filled with so much horsepower and technology.

Check local listing for race telecast on ABC or ESPN.

Our Minds Are Always Racing

DRIVERS
Penskes from heaven

By David Phillips

Some matches are made in heaven: Lennon and McCartney, Astair and Rogers, Rice and Taylor…Penske and Unser. Before 1994, Roger Penske and the Unser family had teamed-up for two PPG titles, a pair of Indianapolis 500 victories and a total of 14 IndyCar wins.

But in his first season with Marlboro Penske Racing, Al Unser Jr. redefined the Penske/Unser relationship with the most dominating performance in the 15 year history of the PPG Indy Car World Series. In one fell swoop, Al added eight wins, another Indy 500 triumph—

Penske's tenth—and a third PPG Championship to the Penske/Unser legacy.

But Unser wasn't the only contributor to the orgy of Penske wins in 1994. Teammates Emerson Fittipaldi and Paul Tracy combined for four more victories to bring Marlboro Penske's 1994 total to 12—a single season record for one team—and participated in no less than five 1-2-3 finishes, six if you count the final PPG points standings which showed Unser at 225, Fittipaldi at 178 and Tracy at 152 some 38 points clear of the nearest challenger.

The season opener gave little hint of what was to come. While Michael Andretti and Nigel Mansell battled for supremacy along Australia's Gold Coast, Unser and Tracy went out early and with little fanfare. After Mansell spun out of contention, Fittipaldi served as the meat in an Andretti sandwich as Michael brought his new Reynard chassis home in first and Mario came home third to share the victory podium for the 16th (and final time) in their storied IndyCar careers.

But if the Penske competition was

better prepared for the first race of the season, it was with good reason. In addition to preparing for Surfers Paradise and the other "spring" races with the regulation 2.65 overhead cam Ilmor D engine, Penske and Ilmor, together with Mercedes-Benz, had been hard at work developing a 209 cubic inch push-rod engine to meet the unique rules package for the Indianapolis 500 in May. Allotted 22% more turbo boost than the overhead cam engines, the Mercedes 209I was expected to have anywhere from a one to two hundred horsepower advantage at the Brickyard.

So while the rest tested with a single purpose in mind, Penske was necessarily divided in its focus. And if the dual programs compromised the effort a bit in Australia, by Phoenix the Penske machine was firing on all cylinders. There Tracy took pole from impressive rookie Jacques Villeneuve to make it an all-Canadian front row, while Fittipaldi and Unser qualified sixth and ninth, respectively.

And while Tracy sprinted to an impressive lead, he was unwittingly involved in a grinding crash between Teo Fabi and Hiro Matsushita, leaving Fittipaldi and Unser to romp to a Penske 1-2 a full lap clear of Mansell. A week later, Unser took a typically heady win at Long Beach (his fifth win on Chris Pook's turf) by babying his gearbox after those of his teammates broke under the strain of the stop-and-go circuit and it was on to Indianapolis.

As predicted, the Mercedes-powered Penskes dominated the month of May. Fastest through much of practice, the Penskes were a good bet to monopolize the front row before Tracy crashed on Friday afternoon and was denied medical clearance to qualify on Pole Day. Somewhat surprisingly, it was Unser—never known as an especially strong qualifier—who took pole at 228.011 mph while Raul Boesel bumped Fittipaldi down to third spot with a 227.618 to his countryman's 227.303. Villeneuve again underlined his potential by taking the inside of the second row ahead of Michael Andretti and an impressive Lyn St. James, while Mansell headed an illustrious third row alongside Arie Luyendyk and Mario Andretti. Tracy would start from the last row after qualifying on the second weekend.

Unser and Fittipaldi left Boesel in the dust long before the green flag with Emmo quickly asserting himself on a day he would dominate. And though Michael Andretti, Mansell and Villeneuve gave spirited chase to the two Marlboro Penske Mercedes, it was really no contest. Andretti fell back with a puncture, Mansell was taken out in a bizarre pit road accident and Tracy dropped out with a broken turbo, leaving Villeneuve fighting just to stay on the same lap as Fittipaldi and Unser.

For that matter, even Unser struggled to stay on the lead lap with Fittipaldi. With less than fifty miles to go Emerson put Unser a lap down, only to have Al come steaming past the next time around. Trying to put the nail in Unser's coffin on lap 184, Emerson tried to get a run on his teammate approaching the pit straightaway. But the Brazilian clipped the inside curb, rebounded into the outside wall and the race was Al's—his second Indy 500 win in three years.

Relieved to get back to what was expected to be a level playing field, the competition arrived in Milwaukee for what was, in a sense, the final weekend to harbor any illusions about the fundamental nature of the 1994 PPG Indy Car World Series. By Saturday afternoon, the lineup featured Boesel on pole for the second year in a row followed by Tracy, Robby Gordon, Villeneuve, Scott Goodyear, Dominic Dobson and impressive rookie Bryan Herta. With Fittipaldi eighth and Unser eleventh, it shaped up as anybody's race.

And it WAS anybody's race—anybody driving Marlboro Penske PC23-Ilmors. As Phoenix had hinted, while the PC23 may not have enjoyed a dramatic edge on the Lolas and Reynards over a qualifying lap or two, it was an exceptionally consistent machine over the 60-70 mile runs between pit stops on race day. So while the Lolas and Reynards could match the Penskes in qualifying, for the first few laps of the race and after a pit stop for fresh tires, within ten or fifteen laps the balance on those cars was gone while the Penskes sailed serenely on.

Race day saw Tracy shoot straight into the lead as Fittipaldi and Unser moved smartly through the field. Fittipaldi swept past Tracy into the lead on lap 23 only to have Unser repeat the maneuver eight laps later and motor away into the distance. Al would give up the lead only during the pit stop shuffling and headed a Penske 1-2-3 when rain stopped the race after 192 laps. Unser and Fittipaldi finished two laps ahead of Tracy who was himself a lap clear of a frenetic scramble for fourth between Michael Andretti, Nigel Mansell and Robby Gordon that went to the Pennsylvanian.

Detroit would prove the PC23's virtues were not limited to the ovals. Only Tracy's slight indiscretion of nudging Unser off course as they jousted for the lead stood between the team and a second straight 1-2-3. Penske's second 1-2-3 would have to wait until Portland, where Unser led an on-form Fittipaldi home ahead of Tracy. Cleveland was the next to fall to the Penske juggernaut with Al winning his fourth of the season with Mansell at least edging Tracy for second place after Fittipaldi fell out of third.

In a year where so much had gone right for Penske, it was almost inevitable that things had to go wrong sometime. Those times arrived in Toronto and

Michigan. Unser was the second retirement in Toronto while Tracy went down a lap with a cut tire, leaving Fittipaldi to keep the team's string of podium finishes alive with a third place behind Michael Andretti and an on-form Bobby Rahal. More trouble lay in wait for the Marlboro threesome at Michigan where first Tracy fell out with fuel pressure problems, then Fittipaldi blew up, leaving Unser to duke it out with Boesel in a contest that would ultimately see both drivers retire with broken engines, and a delighted Goodyear come home to a surprise win from Arie Luyendyk and Dobson.

Though Unser came up empty in Canada and Michigan, the numbing attrition at MIS meant none of his challengers in the PPG points race gained appreciable ground. So at Mid-Ohio, New Hampshire and Vancouver, Al put a stranglehold on his second PPG title with three more victories. His Mid-Ohio win came only after Tracy had been assessed a controversial stop-and-go penalty for passing Gordon under a yellow flag, while Al beat Fittipaldi at New Hampshire in a tense strategic battle after the Brazilian stormed back from early tire problems to lead the race, only to be forced to make a splash-and-go fuel stop five laps shy of the finish.

But Al saved his most amazing win of the season for last. Suffering from food poisoning when he arrived in Vancouver, Unser never even made it to the track on Friday and qualified eighth fastest only after taking on fluids intravenously. By no means 100% on Sunday and in a points-collecting mode, Al approached the race in a circumspect frame of mind.

It was just the ticket for yet another win. While more aggressive drivers took turns bouncing off one another and Vancouver's unyielding walls, Al drove his own race. When a couple of full course yellows played into his hands, Unser was home free from Gordon and Michael Andretti as Mansell torpedoed Fittipaldi out of fourth place in a last turn collision.

Al took his eight for twelve record to Road America with a good shot at clinching the 1994 PPG title as well as taking another step towards either matching (or surpassing) the record for wins in a single season—ten—held by his father and A.J. Foyt. For Unser, the bad news is that he came up just three car lengths short of win number nine. The good news is that his second place, coupled with Fittipaldi's third, secured his second PPG title and Penske's ninth IndyCar championship. And good news for the IndyCar racing community as a whole came from the fact that the man who bested Al was 23 year old Jacques Villeneuve, surely the most impressive "pure" rookie to tackle IndyCar racing since the days of Michael Andretti and Al Unser Jr. himself.

The title decided, the teams arrived

on Penske's home turf at Nazareth for the final short oval of the season—and Mario Andretti's final hometown appearance. Although Mario went out early after tangling with Eddie Cheever, it was another monster day for the home team as Tracy showed a clean pair of heels to Unser and Fittipaldi to lead the team's fifth 1-2-3 sweep of 1994 fully four laps ahead of Boesel, who himself was another lap clear of the fifth placed Stefan Johansson.

Tracy went to Laguna Seca all but certain that the final race of 1994 would also be his swan song at Penske. Successful as the three car package had been, Penske and Marlboro were not inclined to commit the resources necessary to mount a reprise of their three-pronged assault on the 1994 season in the years to come. Like Danny Sullivan in 1990, Tracy found himself the odd man out in a Penske downsizing. And just as Sullivan had done four years earlier, Tracy exited on a triumphant note by storming to a dominant win—his third of the season—to clinch third in the points.

It was a difficult year for Tracy but one he ultimately handled with laudable maturity. Effectively shut out of the points until Milwaukee, Paul saw his role as the future of Penske Racing usurped by Unser during the course of the season. But at year's end Tracy scored a dominant win at Nazareth, impressed observers on both sides of the Atlantic in a test with the Benetton F-1 team, won going away at Laguna Seca and, finally, signed on with Newman/Haas Racing for what promises to be a powerful partnership with Michael Andretti.

Even with the loss of Tracy, Penske retains one of the sport's most powerful lineups. Already one of IndyCar racing's premier drivers, Unser took his talents to a new level this year backed by the unparalleled depth and expertise at Marlboro Penske. And it is no exaggeration to say that 1994 was only a hint of what may lie ahead for the Penske/ Unser relationship.

At age 48 it can also be said with some assurance that the best seasons of Emerson Fittipaldi's career are behind him. But that in no way diminishes the impact his unique blend of experience and passion can still have on any given weekend or season. Quietly, if not silently, Fittipaldi has taken over Rick Mears' role as annual favorite at Indianapolis. But for a blistered tire in 1990 and this year's costly bobble, he could be going for his fifth win in 1995, and he remains a feared contender even as the half century mark looms.

First in the "un-Penske" class, fourth overall, were Michael Andretti and Chip Ganassi Racing. This was a crucial season for Andretti and Ganassi, not to mention Reynard Racing Cars, which became the first new chassis manufac-

turer to enter IndyCar racing in force in more than a decade. And though 1994 could not be considered an unqualified success by any stretch of the imagination, Andretti, Ganassi and Reynard all achieved some measure of what they needed.

Andretti scored an emotional win in Australia—beating Mansell mano-y-mano in the process—to instantly put all the bad thoughts of his miserable 1993 F-1 season behind him. The win was Ganassi's first since taking full control of his team in 1990 and was just reward for faithful sponsors Target stores and Scotch Videos. And it also carried-on Reynard's remarkable legacy of winning its debut race in every major category in which it has competed.

Little could Andretti, Ganassi and Reynard have known what a blessing the Surfers win would be, for the next few months were difficult ones and it wasn't until July—at Toronto—that they would make their second trip to the top of the rostrum. In the final analysis, there were three more races Andretti might have won—Indianapolis, Michigan, and Vancouver. Together with Mansell, Michael was the only driver capable of threatening the Penskes at Indy; after Mansell went out at Michigan the race was Andretti's—until he crashed when Tracy slowed in front of him for a yellow; and he had probably the fastest car on the track at Vancouver but finished third after a series of misfortunes and midadventures.

Those races aside, Andretti and the Ganassi team struggled—at times pathetically—to even stay in the same time zone, not just with the Penskes but with the other top teams. It's true the basic understeer characteristic of the Reynard didn't favor Andretti's style— "the harder he tried the slower he went— but it was also a case of chickens coming home to roost as Michael and the team were intensely secretive about information—even with their own teammate Mauricio Gugelmin—until they were in trouble—and by then it was too late.

Speaking of Gugelmin, the likable Brazilian had a worthy first full season of IndyCar racing, qualifying in the top 10 no fewer than ten times and starting from fifth spot in Detroit and Mid-Ohio— all on a budget that paled in comparison to that of his teammate. Fast and stylish in qualifying, Mauricio seemed to lack aggression in the races proper and was generally off the pace on the ovals, although the virtual absence of testing was surely a factor on that score.

Though a breakthrough win proved elusive, Robby Gordon was a force throughout the season and, with noteworthy support from Walker Racing, emerged as the year's featured Lola-chassied driver. Poles in Toronto and Vancouver stand out of course, but also forceful drives in both races before strik-

ing trouble. Then there was Phoenix, where Robby stayed with the Penskes and led before a costly fuel miscalculation. And how about Michigan? First he controlled his car under duress after blowing a tire at 220 mph then demonstrated his sterling car control a second time, while spinning in the oil of his own blown engine. But perhaps the most impressive aspect of Gordon's season was the fact that he made tangible progress towards becoming a driver who can win races with his brain not just his right foot.

That IndyCar racing is in the midst of a golden era of new talent is underlined by the fact that Jacques Villeneuve joined the likes of Tracy and Gordon as one of the sport's Coming Men. Backed by a solid group of veterans at Forsythe-Green Racing, Villeneuve impressed immediately with a front row qualifying run at Phoenix and a heady second place in the Indianapolis 500. Although Jacques and Forsythe-Green suffered a mild mid-season slump, they rebounded with a brilliant win at Road America as Villeneuve outraced Tracy and Unser to the first of what should be many an IndyCar victory.

Raul Boesel is still looking for his first IndyCar win, and came as close as he's ever come this year when he led 117 laps at Michigan before blowing an engine. In his third year with Dick Simon Racing, Raul was also a force on the other ovals—splitting Unser and Fittipaldi on the front row at Indianapolis, winning his second straight pole at Milwaukee and leading the chase at Nazareth—but at season's end took the opportunity to join Rahal/Hogan Racing in 1995.

Nigel Mansell is another man who'll have a change of scenery in 1995. He'll be back in Formula One with the front rank Marlboro McLaren team, his primary competition over much of his career. The former World and IndyCar champ returned to Formula One at the end of the year, scoring his only win of 1994 in the Australian GP. That triumph helped erase what had been a disappointing defense of his 1993 PPG title, as Mansell went from five wins to no wins in 1994 with Newman/Haas Racing. There were opportunities— Australia, Michigan, Vancouver—but he spun out in a battle with Michael Andretti at Surfers Paradise, fell out with mechanical trouble while dominating the Michigan 500, and then was beset by a couple of inopportune full course yellows at Vancouver before taking-out Fittipaldi in a wildly optimistic last corner bid for fourth place.

Teo Fabi will also be in new surroundings next year, having opted to leave Jim Hall Racing to join Gerry Forsythe's new team. Although Teo and the Hall team had a disappointing first half season, from August on the Pennzoil Reynard was a fixture among the cars

TRUE
COLOURS
ALEXANDER
JULIAN

COLOURS
by
ALEXANDER JULIAN

chasing—albeit futilely—the Marlboro Penskes. Fabi's fourth place at Michigan may have been a gift but he either qualified or finished in the top seven in every race from New Hampshire on to claim ninth in the PPG points.

1994 was like deja vu all over again for Bobby Rahal and the Rahal/Hogan team. For the second year, running uncompetitive equipment negated one of IndyCar racing's top teams. Last year it was the Rahal/Hogan chassis, this year it was the new Honda Indy V-8 engine. Underpowered, heavy and not all that reliable, the various iterations of the Honda were a severe handicap to Rahal and teammate Mike Groff on all but the twistiest of circuits. With non-qualification staring them in the face at Indianapolis—again—the team switched to '93 Penske-Ilmors and was rewarded with a fine third place run by Rahal, while Bobby also scored a brilliant second place in Toronto with Honda power. Groff got off to a good start but slumped after Indianapolis. Rarely afforded the luxury of running the latest engines, he scored just four points from June to October.

Stefan Johansson, Scott Goodyear, and Adrian Fernandez all had their moments, but on the whole had trouble generating momentum. Johansson and the Bettenhausen team got out of the gate with a fourth and fifth, added another fifth in Cleveland, but went through a dry spell that ended with yet another fifth at Nazareth. Goodyear suffered a hideous season with Budweiser/King Racing and for the second time in his career had to take over a teammate's car just to start the Indianapolis 500. There would be no repeat of 1992's heroics—at the Brickyard anyway—but Scott persevered for a fortunate win at Michigan—Lola's lone victory in 1994. Fernandez performed admirably, given that the fortunes of Galles Racing had been unexpectedly thrust on his shoulders in the wake of the team's decision to drop Danny Sullivan. Though he made his share of mistakes, there were also enough instances when his talent showed through—fourth on the grid in Australia, a fifth place at Road America and set to take the lead at Vancouver when the fuel ran out—to hope for good things from Adrian in 1995.

Mario Andretti can also expect good things in 1995, the first year of his retirement from IndyCar racing. He will be driving in selected endurance races in an effort to add some jewels such as the 24 Hours of Daytona and Le Mans to his overflowing trophy case. As for 1994, it was a rewarding if not completely satisfying end to a glorious career that featured 52 wins, 66 poles and four national championships. Although Mario wasn't as consistently competitive as he—and we—would have liked, he did make it onto the podium at Surfers Paradise and qualified in the top

ten 11 of 16 times. He was shaping up as a potential winner at Michigan until he too blew an engine and capped-off his career with an heroic comeback drive at Laguna Seca that ended prematurely with mechanical problems.

Jimmy Vasser, Arie Luyendyk, and Dominic Dobson experienced seasons of fluctuating fortunes although—unfortunately—bad luck tended to outweigh the good. Vasser was the sensation of the early season with top fives in Australia and Phoenix and an excellent fourth at Indianapolis before Hayhoe Racing faltered, scoring just an eleventh and a seventh the rest of the way. Luyendyk was recruited to join the Indy Regency team in its sophomore season. He ran strongly early at Indianapolis, came home a delighted second in the Michigan lottery and had perhaps his best race of the year at Laguna Seca when he came back from an early puncture to finish sixth. Dobson was another to make hay at Michigan, bringing the PacWest Lola-Ford home third and also had a strong weekend at New Hampshire—qualifying and finishing sixth. But with the team talking openly to Sullivan about 1995, he pressed a bit too hard at times and made more than his fair share of mistakes.

1994 was a largely forgettable season for Mark Smith, Willy T. Ribbs, and Scott Sharp. Smith got off to a rocky start with big crashes in Australia and Phoenix, failed to qualify at Indianapolis and only showed flashes of his promising 1993 form late in the season after he'd decided to retire. Ribbs was punted out of a potential top five finish at Surfers Paradise and, like Smith, failed to make the show at Indy. Like Smith, he had his best finish at Michigan but it was the only time he dented the top ten. Sharp began his rookie season perhaps better than expected, with two points-paying finishes in his first five races, but failed to make any appreciable progress during the course of the year. He usually qualified between 15th and 20th and, when the PacWest car ran all day, finished between 10th and 15th. Quietly.

Hiro Matsushita, Marco Greco, and Buddy Lazier also have little reason to remember 1994 fondly. At least Hiro could count his blessings after escaping unscathed from a monumental accident in Phoenix when Villeneuve drilled the Panasonic car amidships following its tangle with Fabi and Tracy. And like many others, Matsushita was there at Michigan to pick up the pieces with a career-best sixth place. Greco had a generally undistinguished rookie season, the lone bright spot of which was a forceful drive at Long Beach that ended with the Arciero Lola imbedded in a tire wall after running as high as ninth. Lazier's season peaked when he was called on to shake-down Robby Gordon's car in the warm-up at New Hampshire after the Walker driver over-

slept. That Buddy went faster than he had in his own Leader Cards machine in just a handful of laps—and in a car that was later found to be significantly off on its set-up—is an indication of the hand he was dealt the rest of the time.

Bryan Herta, Alessandro Zampedri, and Parker Johnstone made their IndyCar debuts with varying degrees of success. 1993 Firestone Indy Lights Champion Herta took over A.J. Foyt's Lola-Ford at Indianapolis and quickly showed he ranks with Tracy, Gordon and Villeneuve when it comes to the future of IndyCar racing. Seventh on the grid at Milwaukee, he was also in the running at Detroit but his season ended in a grinding crash at Toronto. Still, Chip Ganassi had seen enough to tab him as Michael Andretti's replacement for 1995. Zampedri got off to a rocky start with a couple of shunts at Surfers Paradise but redeemed himself with great drives at Portland and Cleveland. He too was injured in a big crash at Michigan but returned to Dale Coyne's Lola-Ford for the final three races but was not fully up to snuff. Johnstone faced the unenviable task of learning the IndyCar ropes with a "rookie" team—Comptech Racing—and a '93 Lola-Honda. Given that the vastly more experienced Rahal/Hogan team struggled with two veteran drivers and '94 chassis, Parker and Comptech did well just to qualify for the half dozen races they entered.

Veterans Eddie Cheever, Davy Jones, and Andrea Montermini had mixed seasons. After a strong May in one of John Menard's cars, Cheever took over for the injured Herta at Foyt but failed to score points in seven outings. Jones actually began the season with Foyt, but crashed in Australia and Phoenix and parted company with Foyt after scoring a point at Long Beach. He qualified a second Bud/King car at Indianapolis, only to be told to stand down for Scott Goodyear on race day. Montermini was fifth fastest and on a quicker lap at Surfers when he crashed the Project Indy Lola. He returned to drive the second Bud/King car in Cleveland and Toronto, taking seventh in Canada, before finishing the year with Project Indy at Laguna Seca.

Christian Danner and Franck Freon also drove the Project Indy Lola, with the underrated Danner earning a PPG point at both Detroit and Road America, doubling Freon's score from his Long Beach appearance.

John Andretti was yet another man to drive for Foyt in 1994, qualifying and finishing tenth at Indianapolis in between flights to his "day job" in NASCAR at Sears Point and Charlotte. Roberto Guerrero also made a single start at Indianapolis but was the first retiree while Stan Fox was the race's final retiree after qualifying Ron Hemelgarn's new Reynard thirteenth and running well up into the top ten.

1. New Champion…**Al Unser Jr.**, winner of half the races, one quarter of the poles, and the Indianapolis 500.
Swift, smart, secure.

Steve Swope

2. Strong Second Place…**Emerson Fittipaldi**, a rare miscue while in the lead cost him a third Indianapolis 500. lowered his momentum in the title chase.

David Taylor

3. The Third Penske Player...**Paul Tracy**, making up for a slow start, lost none of his speed, displayed new found maturity, ran away with the season's last two races.

Cheryl Day Anderson

David Taylor

4. Back Home Again...**Michael Andretti** returned to familiar IndyCar turf with a win in the season opener, followed with a second in Toronto, to become the only non-Penske multiple winner of the year.

Ron McQueeney

5. Fastest Non-Winner...**Robby Gordon**'s two poles and several near misses while in potentially race-winning situations, mark him as a driver who will not long be denied a first victory.

Cheryl Day Anderson

6. Purest New Talent...**Jacques Villeneuve** overcame a heart stopping early season accident to win a race (Road America) after placing second at the Indianapolis 500. '94 Rookie of the Year.

Brian Leshon

7. Up Front on the Ovals…**Raul Boesel**, just missed an elusive first victory at Michigan after leading 117 laps. On the front row at Indianapolis, on the pole at Milwaukee, his speed is amply documented.

8. Returning to Formula One…**Nigel Mansell**, the '93 PPG Cup champion started the '94 season in high style, repeating his pole position in Australia. After that, every bounce went the wrong way, including the one that put Dennis Vitolo's car atop his pit bound Lola in the Indy 500. He won the final Formula One race of the year from the pole.

David Taylor

9. Strong Second Half...**Teo Fabi** managed to turn around a lustre-less early season with a strong second half performance that put him well within the year's top ten.

Brian Leshon

10. Proven Driver, Problem Car...**Bobby Rahal**'s just barely in the top ten season is truly a testimonial to his skill and perseverance. Third place in the Indy 500 in a rented car and second in Toronto in his disappointing Lola Honda were highlights of a year not up to his normal standards.

Bob Steig

11.

Not Quite Top Ten...**Stefan Johansson**'s strong season start and finish bookended a less productive mid-season.

12.

Marlboro 500 Winner...**Scott Goodyear** outlasted an attrition decimated Michigan field for his and Lola's only win of the season.

Ron McQueeney

13.

Promising Newcomer...**Adrian Fernandez** performed admirably as Galles Racing's no. 1 driver, a spot he inherited when established star Danny Sullivan was dismissed.

14.

Arrivederci Mario...**Mario Andretti**, the Driver of the Quarter Century, closed out a distinguished IndyCar career. Twice in position to challenge for the win he suffered mechanical failure. A tearful podium appearance with son Michael in Australia was the highlight of his last PPG Cup campaign.

Brian Leshon

15.

Strong Start…**Jimmy Vasser**, the STP standard bearer, jumped off to a fast '94 start with three top fives in the first four events.

Dan Bianchi

16.

Talented No. 2…**Mauricio Gugelmin** made the most of no. 2 status in the Chip Ganassi camp, demonstrating talent worthy of further development.

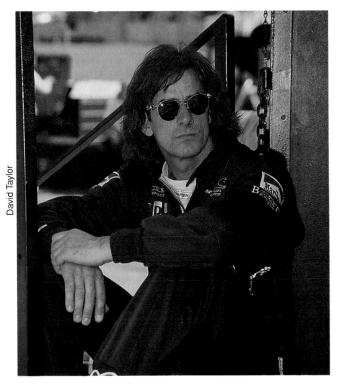

David Taylor

17.

At Home on the Speedways…**Arie Luyendyk**, showed his 1990 Indianapolis winning form in the early stages of the '94 500, garnered second place at Michigan, finished the year with a commendable sixth place at Laguna Seca.

18.

On the Podium at Michigan...**Dominic Dobson**'s third place in the Marlboro 500 at Michigan was his best ever placement.

19.

Early Retiree...**Mark Smith** produced his best results late in the season, after he'd already announced his retirement.

20.

Rahal's no. 2...**Mike Groff** had the unenviable role of being the no. 2 driver in a team with essentially uncompetitive equipment, still managed to squeak into the top twenty.

JACQUES VILLENEUVE
and the genetics of speed

By Lewis Franck

Steve Mohlenkamp

It has never been an easy task to compete with a famous father's reputation. Ask Al Unser, Jr. or Michael Andretti. On the other hand, if speed is really in your genes does your father's reputation matter?

This year Jacques Villeneuve, another son of a lengendary driver, rocketed on the IndyCar scene, winning his first race, a monumental second place at the Indy 500, and the Rookie of the Year title. It wasn't all easy. The 23 year old son of the late Ferrari Formula One hero, Gilles Villeneuve, had to storm back after a heart stopping crash at Phoenix to earn the respect of his peers. While his IndyCar success has been quick, he might have chosen another sport.

"I was born in racing, raised in racing. It was a world I could understand," he explained. "I have always loved speed and driving and being on the edge; so it was just natural. But I could have as easily gone into ski racing, motorcross, or anything fast. It was just more natural going into car racing."

One of the hurdles involved in following in his father's footsteps was that there was no room to be bad. He had to be good from the first green flag drop.

Of all the places to start a professional career, he chose the highly competitive Italian Formula Three series, in the country that has elevated the memory of his late father to something resembling reverence.

He shrugged off the spotlight philosophically, "that would have been the case, a little bit, anywhere. What was difficult was not carrying the name itself. Once you get experience and you're fast, then it's okay. Usually, when you are in your first years of racing, you don't do anything good. Nobody knows who you are, and what you are, so you can do what you want and nobody really cares. Once you start going very fast, you get the eyes of the people on you. In my first race I already had the eyes on me and people expected me to win. Well, like everybody else, you need experience and I needed to make my own stupid mistakes," he said.

Jacques has no illusions about what happened at the beginning of his racing career. "The name opens the door but then they cut you twice as fast if you don't perform right away. If you perform it's okay. But the small, little, mistakes that happen are often weighted quite heavily against you. It is easy to burn yourself."

After racing in Italy, Villeneuve spent a year in the Japanese Formula Three series before talent scouts from Canada's Player's brand spotted the budding star. Barry Green, a championship team manager, wanted to be his own boss and co-founded Forsythe-Green Racing with the intention of starting in Formula Atlantic and working up to an IndyCar effort in 1994.

With sponsorship from Player's, the Forsythe-Green team signed Villeneuve and entered a two-car team in the 1993 Toyota Atlantic series with Claude Bourbonnais as the second driver. Highly regarded engineer, Tony Cicale, formerly with Newman/Hass and the Porsche Indy efforts was another key ingredient.

The team was very competitive, and the teammates battled each other for the series championship until an accident at Trois-Rivieres, Quebec, ended both drivers' title hopes.

For the 1994 season, the team graduated and Villeneuve was entered in the PPG Cup series. No one doubted Villeneuve's potential; it was only a matter of time as to when the results would come. Before the glory came the pain.

Fortunately everybody involved in the Phoenix crash survived with a collective sigh of relief. The Phoenix incident proved to be the defining moment of the season.

One thing established IndyCar drivers fear is a fast driver without experience. Only a really fast driver is going to be racing at the limit and it is so easy to get into trouble at this level.

Paul Tracy and Hiro Matsushita were in their disabled racers at the third turn, when Villeneuve, coming up fast behind some slower cars, crashed into Matsushita's Lola, right behind the cockpit, shearing off the engine and transmission. The flying pieces nearly hit Tracy. Amazingly, there were no serious injuries.

Reflecting on the accident Villeneuve

said, "When you are doing 180 mph at Phoenix, concentrating on traffic, you are at the limit. Going around a corner; if you are just behind the wing of someone, you'll miss the yellow light. We were lucky. It was terrible."

"I never had a doubt. I knew I didn't see the lights, be it my fault, or not. Maybe they were visible and I just didn't see them, well, then I'll take the blame.

But, maybe, they were not very visible. There were cars in front of me that didn't seem to slow down earlier than me, either. It's just one of those things when you go at that speed. The wrong decision and something big happened. And we are lucky that nobody got hurt."

The last thing a rookie, or a new team for that matter, can do is to dwell on past mistakes. Indianapolis loomed a few weeks later, and this was the Broadway opening night for the team. "The Indianapolis 500; the most important sporting event in the world," said Villeneuve respectfully. For budding IndyCar drivers it certainly is.

He got down to business in qualifying; he had to. "You forget about the fact that there are a quarter million people sitting there. All you see is the race track, the walls, and your race car. You completely forget about everything else. All you know is how the car feels and you go out of the pits saying, 'okay, I've got to trust it, keep it floored' and hope for the best. That's what I did. Up to that morning I had never done a flat (full throttle) lap. And that morning I did the four turns without lifting. I knew, okay, in qualifying I'm going to go out and that's what I got to do. And it worked!" Villeneuve qualified at 226.259 mph in fourth starting position.

Now that he was in the show, it was time to prove that he had the maturity to handle the situation. He did just that with flying colors.

While many will remember the Penske dominance, Villeneuve and his team can be very proud. After Penske's feat, Villeneuve's second place was the high point of the race.

"It was a great turning point for us. We needed the lift. It was good to show people that I could do a three and a half hour race without doing anything stupid, by just staying concentrated. Everyone expects young guys to just lose their mind and go crazy. At a race like Indy, it's so important to stay focused. I think, at that place, I showed I could keep my head cool and clear."

His performance at Indianapolis was proof that his rookie errors were well behind him. Now, it was only a matter of time before his first win. It came at Elkhart Lake. That was no small feat, considering that except for the two wins by Michael Andretti and one by Scott Goodyear, the Penskes won everything else.

Was it because his family home was in Monte Carlo he persuaded the team to gamble on a low downforce set-up at Elkhart Lake? Perhaps the European influence was there. "I've always used little downforce, I brought that idea from Italy, where on a few tracks like Monza, we used to run without a rear wing, take off the top wing. It always worked."

"Even if the laptime wasn't quicker, in a race, if you are in front of someone it's very difficult for them to overtake you, if you don't make a mistake. We knew that the Penskes were fast, like everywhere else. We just tried it and it worked."

Villeneuve made a daring pass on Tracy and Unser Jr. at a restart to take the lead and held off his countryman and Unser Jr. for his breakthrough victory.

"When I made that pass I knew that was the best moment to make it. So I just took every chance I had and went for it. Once I was in the lead, I had the two Penskes…in my mirror all the time, until Tracy dropped out. I knew that if I didn't make a mistake in the corner then either Junior or Tracy would have a hard time, to get into the tow, to overtake me because of my lower downforce. Even then, whenever they got closer, I had a feeling that they could actually do something. Until you get your first victory you always expect something to happen for you not to win it, even when you're out front."

"How did it feel? It was a great moment. It felt just the way I was expecting it to feel. I really wanted it. It's not like it came out of nowhere and oh, wow, I've won a race, like winning at a lottery. You work for it," he explained.

There can be no doubt that in his short career Jacques Villeneuve has earned the right to be respected as a fine driver. Modestly, he commented, "I didn't think it would be so fast. The climb has been quite fast. This has been only my sixth year of racing. There was a big learning curve." Speed really must be in the genes.

Steve Mohlenkamp

TEAMS
Marlboro Penske at the top

By David Phillips

Even by Marlboro Penske Racing's lofty standards, 1994 was a remarkable season. That would have been the case if Al Unser Jr. had "only" won eight races and the PPG Indy Car World Series title. But to have Emerson Fittipaldi and Paul Tracy take four more wins between them and bring the team's total to a record 12 made 1994 even more special. And to have Unser, Fittipaldi and Tracy score five 1-2-3 finishes—and finish 1-2-3 in the PPG points—made for a season of unparalleled achievement. Even Penske may have trouble matching it.

Oh by the way, Penske also won its tenth Indianapolis 500 victory, and did so in a fashion that was vintage Roger Penske. Taking advantage of USAC's rules affording pushrod engines 18% more boost (55″ to 45″) and 22% more capacity than conventional 2.65 litre overhead cam engines, Penske and partners Ilmor Engineering and Mercedes-Benz designed, built, tested and developed the Mercedes 209I in eight months. And they did it in total secrecy and without missing so much as a beat on their "other" IndyCar program featuring the Ilmor D engine.

Talk about the unfair advantage. A lot of people did.

But, of course there was nothing "unfair" about the Mercedes. It was built in strict compliance with rules that had been around since 1991. Nor was there anything "unfair" about the way Penske went about winning 11 of the remaining 15 races held outside the Hoosier state. It was simply a case of complete professionalism getting its just desserts.

Where to begin? Begin where all Penske chassis do, on the drawing board at Penske Cars, Ltd. in Poole, England where chief designer Nigel Bennett and his associates penned the PC23 chassis. Although the PC23 was quick enough to capture 10 of 16 poles on the year, its primary advantage lay in the fact that its handling characteristics stayed relatively constant as the fuel load lightened.

Not only were the PC23s fast and consistent, there were more of them than any Penskes since 1990, the last time Marlboro Penske mounted a season-long three car effort. That was not one of the team's better years. Emerson Fittipaldi, Rick Mears, and Danny Sullivan managed just four wins between

them, and even Penske's resources were stretched by the three car program.

For 1994, Penske mounted a complete three car effort, top to bottom. That began at the Penske factory where managing director Teddy Mayer and director and general manager Nick Goozee ran a tight and productive ship overseeing the manufacture (and occasional repair) of chassis. Such was the factory's level of proficiency that, during the winter testing season, new PC23s were shipped directly to the test sites rather than to the race shop in Reading, PA for final assembly.

That efficiency was matched at the team's race shop in Reading, Pennsylvania where, in addition to preparing and maintaining a minimum of five chassis per race weekend Karl Kainhofer and his crew were also once again the only team responsible for servicing the Ilmor D engines.

Team manager Chuck Sprague administered a new team structure that had crew chiefs Rick Rinaman, Jon Bouslog and Richard Buck overseeing the preparation on the cars of Fittipaldi, Tracy, and Unser, respectively, while Grant Newbury served as the team's

chief engineer, coordinating the work of Unser's engineer, Terry Satchell; Fittipaldi's engineer, Tom Brown; and Tracy's engineer, Nigel Beresford.

The record speaks for how well the new organization performed; not just the record number of wins but in other ways as well. Like the fact that Unser won more poles in 1994 than he'd won in the previous 12 years of his IndyCar career; or the fact that the Michigan 500 was the only time all year that a Penske driver wasn't on the rostrum; or the fact that Fittipaldi and Unser completed nearly 200 laps more on the season than their nearest rival...

Chip Ganassi Racing has borne the brunt of much criticism over the years—and the detractors surely were not silent on those occasions when the team struggled in 1994. But when it's all said and done, Ganassi won the "non-Penske" class and Michael Andretti was the only driver other than Unser and Tracy to score multiple wins in 1994. And in his first full IndyCar season, Mauricio Gugelmin served notice that he will be heard from in the coming years.

That the Ganassi team accomplished all of that while working with Reynard

Racing Cars in its first year of IndyCar competition—not to mention Michael Andretti's first year with the team and after being away from IndyCar racing for a full season—speaks of the team's talent and professionalism.

As he has since Chip Ganassi took control of the team in 1990, Tom Anderson served as an effective team manager while Mike Hull, who joined the team in 1991, worked as crew chief on Andretti's car. New to the Ganassi organization in 1994, cheerful John Bright was in charge of Gugelmin's car and more than once outshone the "A" team in practice and qualifying. Julian Robertson, who joined Ganassi in mid-1993, continued on as chief engineer while Morris Nunn, whose ties with Ganassi date back to their days at Patrick Racing, came on board in July and quickly contributed to Andretti's win in Toronto.

Of course, it's no coincidence that Andretti's win at Surfers Paradise kept alive Reynard's streak of winning in every major category in which it's competed. The Reynard 95I, designed by a team led by Malcolm Oastler was a worthy—and durable—first effort at creating a chassis capable of running laps at 220 mph on the speedways as well as the 80 mph laps on the street circuits.

On the whole, Forsythe-Green Racing was probably the most consistent Reynard team in 1994, and was rewarded with a fine win at Road America in its rookie season. Though the organization itself was new to IndyCar racing, the majority of the key personnel were not. Gerry Forsythe and Barry Green, for example, nearly won the 1983 PPG Indy Car World Series when Teo Fabi took the sport by storm with the Forsythe Brothers

Steve Mohlenkamp

March. Forsythe and Green had joined forces again in 1993 in a quest for the Toyota Atlantic title that also served as preparation for the 1994 IndyCar season with driver Jacques Villeneuve.

The team moved from Toyota Atlantics to IndyCars largely intact, with Barry's brother Kim coming over from Hall Racing as team manager while Kyle Moyer again served as chief mechanic on the Player's car. And as he had been in 1993, engineer Tony Cicale was Forsythe-Green's real ace in the hole, having developed an extraordinarily productive relationship with Villeneuve. Successful as the team was, however, it was not a story of complete and utter harmony as the season ended with Forsythe and Green parting company over "differences in management philosophy."

Nor was 1994 exactly a study in har-

mony for IndyCar racing's other winning team, Budweiser/King Racing. Although new recruit Scott Goodyear posted promising times in winter testing, the Budweiser Lola-Ford was off the pace once the season began. In fact, Goodyear himself failed to qualify for the Indianapolis 500 and the team avoided a major embarrassment only when Davy Jones put their backup car in the show.

Veteran team manager/engineer John Dick joined the team in June and slowly—imperceptibly at times—the Bud/King car's performance improved. Dick and engineer David Benbow formed an effective working relationship while chief mechanic Joe Flynn and his crew usually gave Goodyear a car that would run to the finish. That was certainly the case when the team scored a surprise win in the attrition-filled Michigan 500—Lola's only win in 1994—but a look at the last half of the season shows that Scott was in the points in six of eight races.

In the final analysis, however, Budweiser, the No. 1 beer brand, was looking for more than one fortuitous win and 12th in the PPG points, and subsequently joined forces with Newman/Haas Racing for '95. And after two generally disappointing seasons, team owner Kenny Bernstein closed the doors on his IndyCar operation.

Though victory eluded them, Walker Racing had a successful season in 1994—at least that part of it associated with Robby Gordon's Valvoline Lola-Ford. While Gordon took a pair of poles, led at Phoenix, Toronto, and Vancouver and finished fifth in points, Willy T. Ribbs and Mark Smith rarely figured in the team's other cars. Dick Caron came to Walker in 1994 from Simon Racing to assume the team manager's responsibility—no small task during a season in which the three car team moved from its old home near Philadelphia to a modern

Brian Leshon

facility in Indianapolis.

Dan Miller, Tom Howatt, and Phil Howard worked as chief mechanics for Gordon, Smith, and Ribbs, respectively, while long-time Walker associate Tim Wardrop handled the engineering duties on Gordon's car with notable success and Rob Edwards and veteran Gordon Coppuck worked in the same capacity with Ribbs and Smith.

Dick Simon Racing was another busy team, running cars for Raul Boesel, Hiro Matsushita and, in association with Arciero Racing, Marco Greco, throughout the season, not to mention additional cars for Lyn St. James and Dennis Vitolo at Indianapolis. As usual, Gilbert

appointing eighth in the points race and Mario Andretti could do no better than fourteenth.

Team manager Jim McGee had his hands full during a season when hostilities between his two drivers reached the boiling point on more than one occasion. But if the results were unsatisfactory, it was not for lack of effort. Indeed, with the possible exception of Gordon, Mansell was the only driver capable of regularly matching the pace of the three Penskes and he was unlucky not to win at Michigan and Vancouver in a car engineered by Peter Gibbons and prepared by a crew led by Tom Wurtz. As he has since 1991, Brian Lisles worked as

Larry Ellert and Rob Hill had their work cut out for them, as reliability problems cropped-up with some regularity in the engine department.

Although the end result shows that Hall Racing moved up just two notches in the PPG point standings from 1993— eleventh to ninth—the Midland, Texas-based team had a late season surge that bodes well for 1995. Engine tuner turned team manager Gerald Davis joined the team at the start of the season while most of the other key personnel, including driver Teo Fabi, chief mechanic Alex Hering, and engineer Bill Pappas returned to the fold. While the first half of the season brought indiffer-

Cheryl Day Anderson

Ron McQueeney

Lage handled the team manager's chores but he was joined at mid-year by IMSA-veteran Emory Donaldson in the overall administration of the team while Bob Sprow handled the Arciero operation. The appearance of Donaldson was soon followed by wholesale changes on Matsushita's crew while engineer Morris Nunn left the team soon after Indianapolis to join Ganassi Racing. And though Boesel ultimately opted at season end to leave Simon for a spot at Rahal/Hogan, he did so after taking his second straight pole at Milwaukee, nearly winning at Michigan, and finishing seventh in PPG points.

By any measure, powerful Newman/ Haas Racing had its least successful season since first entering the PPG Indy Car World Series in 1983. For the first time ever, the Newman/Haas cars failed to win a race, as 1993 PPG champion Nigel Mansell finished a dis-

Mario Andretti's engineer while John Simmonds was crew chief on the Andretti Kmart/Texaco Lola-Ford which made the podium in Australia and was looking a potential winner at Michigan when the engine failed.

Rahal/Hogan Racing had another difficult season, thanks to the teething problems associated with the new Honda Indy engine. Scott Roembke and Jim Prescott administered the team's expansion to a full time two car effort and though the cars of Bobby Rahal and Mike Groff struggled on the straightaways, Rahal in particular was as quick as anyone through the corners —despite usually running with a bare minimum of downforce. That speaks well of the work done by Rahal and engineer Tim Reiter, while Groff and Bernie Marcus, and later Ray Leto, also made the Motorola Honda go quicker than it had a right to at times. Chief mechanics

ent results, after a serendipitous fourth place at Michigan, the team began generating some positive momentum and either qualified or finished in the top seven in five of the last six races.

Galles Racing embarked on a major rebuilding program in 1994, first scaling down to a one car team after running as many as three cars the previous season. With Al Unser Jr. heading to Penske, Danny Sullivan was expected to carry the Galles standard with support from Adrian Fernandez, but a late decision by Rick Galles to part company with the 1988 PPG champ—one that left Sullivan high and dry for 1994—thrust the team's fate on Fernandez' shoulders.

Adrian responded well, with noteworthy support from Ed Nathman, who'd rejoined the team in a dual role as team manager and engineer in 1993 after a successful stint with Newman/Haas. Nathman concentrated on the engineer-

ing side in 1994, enabling veteran crew chief Owen Snyder to assume the team manager's role while Mitch Davis took over as chief mechanic on the Tecate/Quaker State Reynard. Although the team failed to win a race for the first time since 1987, Fernandez & Co. laid a solid foundation for better times in 1995.

Tony Bettenhausen Racing continued the process of building a quality small team, and for the third year in a row moved up in the season standings. Indeed, but for a disastrously controversial pit stop at Laguna Seca that led to a couple of stop-and-go penalties, Stefan Johansson would have earned Bettenhausen its first top ten finish in the PPG points. As it is, team manager Joe Ward and chief mechanic Steve Ritenour saw to it that the Alumax Penske PC22-Ilmor was good for ten finishes in 16 starts (and fifth best in miles completed). And the team's fortunes were bolstered by the addition of engineer Ken Anderson to the roster. As a sign of the team's increasing depth, Bettenhausen entered a second car at Long Beach and Portland for Robert Groff, who finished just out of the points on both occasions.

After several seasons running either in association with other teams or on a limited basis, Hayhoe Racing struck out on its own in 1994 and looked sensational —for a while. But after a fourth place at Indianapolis the results plummeted, more as the result of misfortune and a financial shortfall than shortcomings on either the part of driver Jimmy Vasser or the Phil Casey-led crew. Engineer David Cripps frequently helped Vasser arrive at a competitive set-up—until the testing budget vanished—while Randy Bain came on board as chief mechanic at mid-season to help lighten the load on Casey. But points were few and far between from June through October and, after learning that principle sponsor Conseco would not return in 1995, Hayhoe ultimately forged a new alliance with Ganassi for the coming season.

Indy Regency was another team to have its moments but, ultimately, never reach its potential largely as the result of insufficient funding to do the job. Owner/team manager Sal Incandella was instrumental in bringing 1990 Indy 500 winner Arie Luyendyk on board for the team's second season but the team went through a number of changes in personnel during the course of the summer, with Daryl Fox assuming the role of chief mechanic and Brian Berthold taking over for Ian Ashdowne on the engineering side. Luyendyk ran well in the opening burst at Indianapolis and was in the midst of a storming drive at Cleveland when his engine let go, thus the team had to be content with a fortuitous second place at Michigan and an underrated sixth at Laguna Seca for its highlights.

After appearing in a handful of races in 1993, the PacWest Racing Group made a big splash in 1994 with a two car effort for Dominic Dobson and two time Trans-Am champ Scott Sharp. Although the flanks of the PacWest Lola-Fords were rarely sullied by the appearance of sponsorship logos, lack of funding was not an immediate concern owing to the deep pockets of the ownership consortium consisting of Bruce McCaw, Wes Lamatta, and Tom Armstrong, together with minority partners Dobson and Alan Mertens.

Mertens, the former engineering director for Galles and Galles/Kraco, joined the team over the winter and with him came a useful association with his Galmer Engineering firm, including engineer Andy Brown. Meanwhile, veteran team manager John Anderson was lured away from Foyt Racing, while other key recruits included chief mechanics Paul "Ziggy" Hargus and Mark Moore. The net result was an 18th place finish in the PPG points by Dobson while Sharp finished 21st in a season highlighted by Dobson's second place at Michigan.

After finishing tenth in the PPG points in 1993, A.J. Foyt saw his team stripped of some of its best people in the off-season, beginning with driver Robby Gordon and including team manager John Anderson and his (unrelated) chief engineer Ken Anderson. Compounding the difficulties was the fact that Foyt's original choice as a driver—Davy Jones—didn't work out and the team found itself looking for another pilot for Indianapolis. They found him in Bryan Herta and the 1993 Firestone Indy Lights champion, Foyt, team manager Tom LaMance and chief mechanic Craig Baranouski instantly clicked. Seventh on the grid at Milwaukee, as high as third during the race at Detroit, this was a team going places before Herta's season-ending accident in Toronto. Though it took some time for the team's third driver of the year—Eddie Cheever—to get going, by Nazareth and Laguna Seca he was also running very well. Unfortunately, he was taken out in a crash at Nazareth and dropped out while running in the top five at Laguna Seca.

Dale Coyne Racing had an up and down season, highlighted by Alessandro Zempedri's fine seventh place finish in Portland but blighted by Zempedri's subsequent accident during practice for the Michigan 500. Caused by a cut tire, the crash cost Coyne one '93 Lola and the services of a promising driver, as the congenial Italian was sidelined for six weeks with a cracked pelvis and never really returned to form in the final three events in which he participated. Coyne also ran an aging '92 Lola-Chevy for Ross Bentley but the car was rarely fast enough to qualify. As always, Bernie Myers headed up the mechanical effort with support while David Morgan and Coyne worked on the engineering side of things.

A number of other teams participated in the 1994 season. Bob Lazier teamed-up with Ralph Wilkie to carry the Leader

Card standard. Veteran Paul Diatlovich was brought on board to prepare the team's '93 Lola-Chevy but try as they might, neither Buddy Lazier nor Giovani Lavaggi was able to score a point in the Financial World-backed car. Also making every race—at least physically—was Antonio Ferrari's Euromotorsports team. But after a deal at the Indianapolis 500 came apart the team limped from weekend to weekend, offering Jeff Wood scant opportunity to practice let alone qualify or race in a professional fashion.

On a brighter note, the small Project Indy team didn't make all the races, but they made their presence known when they did. Andrea Montermini looked a sure shot to qualify in the top ten before crashing heavily at Surfers Paradise, but Franck Freon brought team owners Andreas Leberle, Rainer Buhmann, and Christian Danner a PPG point at Long Beach. Danner himself got another point at Road America and the woefully underutilized Montermini scored the team's best finish of the season with a ninth place at Laguna Seca.

Hard trying Dennis McCormack fielded a '93 Lola-Ford for both Frederik Ekblum and Claude Bourbonnais on a few occasions, with veteran chief mechanic Laurie Garrish overseeing affairs in the latter part of the season. Although McCormack's team made five races, neither Bourbonnais nor Ekblum earned a point. Bourbonnais, together with John Paul, Jr., also drove for the ProFormance team owned by Tim Duke and John Dick. Handicapped by aging equipment and a tight budget, though, Bourbonnais and Paul failed to score and the team closed its doors at mid-season.

RINGING IN THE CHANGES
FOR 1995

When one team wins 12 of 16 races and finished 1-2-3 in the PPG points race, it figures the competition will make some big changes. So it's no surprise that the 1995 IndyCar line-up figures to be significantly different from that of 1994.

Headlining the changes is Marlboro Penske's decision to scale back to a two car effort for Al Unser Jr. and Emerson Fittipaldi, with Paul Tracy the odd man out. Not that Tracy fared too badly. After all, he signed-on with Newman/Haas Racing where he will be joined by Michael Andretti as the latter returns to the scene of his greatest success in the wake of a two season leave with the McLaren F-1 and Ganassi IndyCar teams. Together with Andretti and Tracy, Newman/Haas also adds Budweiser to its stable of sponsors topped, as usual, by Kmart and Texaco.

Andretti's departure paved the way for Ganassi to hire talented young Bryan Herta to drive the Target/Scotch Video Reynard. In addition, all signs point to Ganassi joining forces with Jim Hayhoe in a union that will see Jimmy Vasser drive the team's second car.

And that's just for starters.

After spending the 1994 season in racing-limbo, Danny Sullivan will return to full-time employment as lead driver for a PacWest Racing Group that will also switch from Lola to Reynard

chassis in 1995. Consider also that Raul Boesel will join Bobby Rahal at Rahal/Hogan Racing. And that's not the only new twist to the Rahal/Hogan line-up in 1995. After squandering the past two seasons on ambitious efforts to build their own chassis and campaign new Honda engines, Rahal/Hogan is going back to a tried 'n true Lola-Mercedes/Ilmor package.

With Boesel heading to Rahal/Hogan, Dick Simon has signed F-1 and IMSA veteran Elizeo Salazar to drive one of his '95 Lola-Fords, while Dean Hall will return to IndyCars after a four year absence to drive a second Simon entry and Hiro Matsushita will return for another year with the team.

Other new faces on the IndyCar front will include F3000 standout Gil de Ferran from Brazil, tabbed to drive Jim Hall's Pennzoil Reynard-Ilmor in 1995. Another Brazilian—Andre Ribeiro—will drive for the "new" Tasman Motorsports team. Although new to IndyCar racing, Tasman has utterly dominated the Firestone Indy Lights Championship the past two seasons. Adding further spice to Tasman's effort is the fact that they will be spearheading Honda's sophomore IndyCar season.

While Honda will be focusing primarily on the Tasman team, Comptech Racing is expected to come aboard at Indianapolis to make a two-pronged Honda effort.

The other major news on the engine

front comes from the alliance between Ilmor Engineering and Mercedes-Benz. Although the partnership pulled-off last year's stunning Indianapolis 500 victory —in concert with Penske—the coming season will see Ilmor and Mercedes running the full PPG Indy Car World Series and supplying the Rahal/Hogan, Galles, Hall, Bettenhausen and Indy Regency teams in addition to Penske.

Nor is Tasman the only new team on the IndyCar scene in 1995. With Gerry Forsythe and Barry Green parting company at the end of 1994, Forsythe has formed his own team with Teo Fabi expected to drive. Forsythe will join the burgeoning Reynard contingent and, on the engine front, will join the ranks of Ford's customers including Newman/Haas, Ganassi, Walker, Simon, PacWest and Foyt.

And in perhaps the most significant news of the year, Pat Patrick and Patrick Racing will return to IndyCar competition with Lola-Fords driven by Scott Pruett and underwritten, in part, by Firestone tires. With tight restrictions on chassis and engine development, most observers agree that tires are the single most significant performance variable in IndyCar racing. And Firestone's entry into the 1995 equation should not only give Goodyear some stiff competition, but will likely result in noticeable changes in team tactics in practice and qualifying, not to mention the races themselves.

TRIUMPHANT RETURN
Michael Andretti bags 1994 IndyCar opener

David Taylor

Surprises are standard fare in the Australian IndyCar Grand Prix. Dark horse John Andretti took the first one in 1991, his only IndyCar triumph. In 1993, world champion Nigel Mansell, with not a single IndyCar race under his belt, bested the field in qualifying and in the race, despite a somewhat rocky ride in between. The '94 surprise was not that winner Michael Andretti was fast and fit in his return to the IndyCar arena, his natural hunting ground, but that he posted the win in a new chassis, Reynard, prepped by a Chip Ganassi team which had never before won an IndyCar race. His jump start to the new season did much to erase the somewhat sour taste of his '93 experiment in Formula One.

The start was delayed twice, first by rain and then by a parade lap accident. The third starting attempt was successful, with polesitter Mansell edging Michael, the other occupant of the front row. A totally intense and clearly focused Michael made a "miracle" pass on the outside of the third turn to take command. The green flag waved only briefly as a multiple car accident behind the leaders involved a dozen cars. Principal victims were Bobby Rahal and Raul Boesel, whose cars were instantly disabled. After six laps under yellow, racing resumed with Emerson Fittipaldi the leader, courtesy of Marlboro Team Penske, producers of the best pit stop among the leaders, all of whom stopped to swap rain tires for slicks. Michael got by Fittipaldi and young charger Robby Gordon took Mansell's measure demoting him temporarily to fourth. Mansell turned up the wick and got back by Gordon and Fittipaldi. Gordon's attempt to retaliate ended in the wall. In ardent pursuit of Michael, Mansell spun and lost a lap in the process. Michael was luckier, his incipient spin scattered the tire wall but his Reynard amazingly shrugged off the impact. Afterwards, "I can't believe this thing," said Michael about the incident. "Flying through the air and then taking all those tires with me. I didn't think it was that bad until I came around the next lap and I mean, those tires were scattered all over the place. But it didn't miss a beat, it didn't bend one thing. That Reynard is just strong."

The second half of the race put the spotlight on a new contender for top honors. Mario Andretti up from a lowly 19th qualifying position, went gunning for second place Fittipaldi. He failed to get by, just as Fittipaldi failed to get Michael. When the race was called for darkness 10 laps short of the scheduled distance, an IndyCar first, this running order set the stage for a teary-eyed Andretti reunion on victory podium; Michael the winner, Mario third, and '93 winner Fittipaldi a strong second. STP-backed Jimmy Vasser posted a satisfying fourth place.

"This means so much to me," said Michael Andretti, holding back tears. "I went through so much last year. It was a very difficult year for me and my family. But we've worked hard this winter, and I prayed to God that things would work out. The Lord answered my prayers."

The Australian IndyCar Grand Prix got the new season off to a high voltage start, a fitting opener to a new IndyCar year with plenty of surprises to come.

MARLBORO TEAM PENSKE
tops the charts at Phoenix

Steve Swope

Emerson Fittipaldi and Al Unser Jr. swept the top two positions for Marlboro Team Penske in the Slick 50 200. It could just as easily have been one-two-three. Polesitter teammate Paul Tracy, running free and clear in the lead, with nary a pursuer visible in his mirrors, managed to crash, while avoiding the wrecked cars of Hiro Matsushita and Teo Fabi. Jacques Villeneuve and Dominic Dobson were caught up in the incident and out for the day. Luckily, no drivers were injured. Matsushita's escape was a near miracle. Robby Gordon lost out on a strong bid for his first IndyCar win by running out of fuel after lap 154, having just posted eight laps in the lead.

Third place went to the reigning champion, Nigel Mansell, who was delighted to have survived the race and matched his third place on the starting grid. "I'm happy just to be sitting here talking to you," said Mansell. "I've never experienced anything like this race in my career.

I killed the motor on the first pit stop, but the crew did a great job of getting me going. On the big crash, half a car was flying one way and half a car was flying another. I came along right in the middle of it and didn't know where to go. It was one of the scariest times I've ever had in motor racing."

Stefan Johansson posted a workmanlike performance for fourth place. STP's Jimmy Vasser, in fifth place at the finish almost matched his fourth place season debut in Australia.

Luck deserted the Andretti clan, which occupied two-thirds of the winner's podium in Australia. Mario crashed when a brake rotor exploded. Michael came on the scene, which was partially obscured by blowing sand, and tagged John Paul Jr., knocking a wheel off Paul's car and into the stands. "It's a shame," said Michael. "We were hanging in there and could have gotten some points. I came up on a sandstorm. I thought sand was

blowing across the track. It was blinding, and the next thing I know I saw two cars right in front of me. I came up so fast I couldn't see anything and I nailed one of them."

Fittipaldi and Unser had no challengers in the second half of the race, proceeding swiftly and securely to the checkered flag. Unser said he had no real hope of beating teammate Fittipaldi. "Emerson had his car working very well," said Unser. "I had a little bit too much understeer, and when we were running in clean air, free of traffic, he could pull away from me. Emerson had the quickest car today. He had the race well in hand. But this is the best race I've ever had here at Phoenix."

After the first two rounds of the PPG Cup proceedings, Fittipaldi at 37 points held a handsome lead over Johansson and Vasser, tied for second at 22, with Michael Andretti a point behind this pair at 21, and champion Nigel Mansell checking in at 19 points for fifth place.

UNSER
Owns Long Beach—Again

Marlboro Team Penske teammates Paul Tracy, the '93 winner, Al Unser Jr., a four-time winner, and Emerson Fittipaldi, no stranger to the podium, were the three fastest qualifiers for the Toyota Grand Prix of Long Beach—and the odds-on prerace favorites. The odds makers were right, but it took all of Unser's rare combination of speed, skill, and patience to notch the win, his record setting fifth at Long Beach, his first for Marlboro Team Penske. Polesitter Tracy sprinted away to an early lead with Unser in close but considered pursuit. Tracy's day in the sun lasted only twenty laps, when he spun as a result of transmission problems. Now in the lead, Unser became the pursued, with Fittipaldi looming large in his mirrors. Fittipaldi indeed took the lead, without a fight, on lap 43 however, on the basis of a stop-and-go penalty leveled against Unser for speeding in pit lane. After lap 62, Fittipaldi too, fell victim to the same transmission woes that beset Tracy. Unser now had a clear field, provided he could tame the transmission troubles that dogged his teammates. He could, and did, nursing his suspect gearbox into victory lane.

"Paul squirted away from me at the beginning," said Unser. "I started to get loose, and he started to go away. Emerson got close to me, and I said, 'Man! They've got better cars than me.' Then I saw Paul get loose and Emerson fade a little bit, and I said, 'We've all got the same race car.' Then it was a case of waiting for the traffic. We were going to see how Paul dealt with the traffic."

Current PPG Cup champion NIgel Mansell had his best outing of the new season, inheriting second place after Tracy and Fittipaldi's misfortune. Two-thirds of the way through the race, however, Mansell suffered a tire puncture on the Shoreline Drive front straight. "I'm just glad it happened on the straight and not in a corner," said Mansell. "There was a vibration and then the car wanted to swap ends. It certainly got my attention. By the time I got to the first turn, I was already on the rim." Mansell had to limp around the track to the pits, but was still able to come back to finish second.

Robby Gordon, still earnestly seeking his first IndyCar win, finished third, on the same lap as the winner, felt he might have done bet-

ter had he been more aggressive. "Our strategy today was just like Phoenix last weekend," said Gordon. "I laid back and just watched things happen in front of me. I guess I laid back a little too much. But I didn't want to make any mistakes today in front of all those people."

Polesitter Tracy was understandably disappointed at the mechanical problems that eliminated his chances of a repeat win. "The transmission would get hung-up and start axle-hopping when I was downshifting," said Tracy. "That first spin really hurt because the engine stalled." Tracy was push-started and drove slowly around to the pits to change a flat right rear tire. Later in the race he spun three more times. "We tried to keep going to try to stay in the race, but it kept repeating and the gearbox finally gave up."

With the confidence inherent in his Long Beach win, and his smooth assimilation into Marlboro Team Penske, Unser left California on top of the PPG Cup points chase, with the look of a driver who could be on a roll.

Michael C. Brown

Michael C. Brown

TOYOTA ATLANTIC STAR WILL BE BACK

Two-Time Player's Toyota Atlantic Champion David Empringham plans to campaign for a third title in a row in '95. While many veteran observers consider him already a viable candidate to be the next Canadian IndyCar standout in the tradition of Paul Tracy and Jacques Villeneuve, he's holding out for an offer from a front-line team. He'll continue to hone his skills in the fast, competitive series powered by racing versions of Toyota's twin cam production engine.

AL UNSER JR.
wins his second Indy 500

A rare Emerson Fittipaldi miscue, the most expensive of his long and distinguished career, cost him a secure lead and almost certain victory with only 16 laps left in motoracing's biggest event. Marlboro Team Penske teammate Al Unser Jr., fighting tenaciously to avoid being lapped by Emmo, was the beneficiary of the miscue. Unser vaulted from second place to the lead and became the new almost certain winner as Fittipaldi gyrated into the wall. Between the two, they led 193 of the 200 laps around the fabled 2.5 mile oval. Second place went to the surprising rookie, Jacques Villeneuve, who demonstrated maturity beyond his years as well as a high turn of speed. Michael Andretti finished third on the track, despite two stop-and-go penalties, was dropped to sixth place post-race for a third infraction. He naturally considered the final penalty unjustified. Bobby Rahal, in a year old "rental car" Penske PC22 had a happy ending to a "Month of May" that threatened to be as disastrous as that of '93, when he failed to qualify.

Though the drivers, as usual, got the lion's share of attention, the real news of the 78th Indianapolis 500 was under the engine covers of the three Penskes. Roger Penske, in typical crisp, analytical fashion had commissioned Ilmor to produce pushrod racing engines allowed by the Indianapolis 500 rules to have 3.4 liters displacement against the 2.6 liters allowed the Ilmor and Ford overhead cam engines. The pushrod engines were additionally allowed 55 inches of turbo boost against 45 for the overhead cam competition. Mercedes-Benz paid development costs and enjoyed the privilege of its logo on the cam covers.

If the Mercedes-Benz engines could last 500 miles, they would run roughshod over the opposition. They could, and did. (To be sure, they had been tested for 500 mile runs.) The advantage in horsepower was conservatively estimated at 100, and the edge in torque was clearly visible. The engines performed

flawlessly in the race for Unser and Fittipaldi, while Tracy's car fell to turbocharger problems, after qualifying six miles per hour slower than pole-sitter Unser. Penske's big gamble proved a smash success, once again reinforcing his position as the country's most astute racing mind.

Where was current PPG Cup champion Nigel Mansell, whose '93 debut at Indianapolis was spectacular, despite being out accelerated by winner Fittipaldi in a late race restart? Doing rather nicely by lap 93, up from seventh at the start to third place, and first in the non-Mercedes-Benz class. He serenely turned into the pit entrance for a routine stop only to have Dennis Vitolo's careening, airborne car land on his engine cover seconds later. It seems Vitolo had misjudged his speed, tagged John Andretti's car from the rear, became airborne, and

bounced atop Mansell's car. To call Mansell merely "disgusted" would involve more British understatement than even he could muster. "Vitolo was going miles too quick and he only braked too late and the next thing he knew he was on top of me. What can I say? I was just following everyone else slowly around in the slip road to the pit entrance. The next thing I know, I'm sort of going half-backwards with a car on top of me, on fire."

"I'm just disappointed. We got back up to third place. Everything was looking good. We were going to get back on the same lead lap. There's no words to express the disappointment and the surprise. I've never had an accident when you've been under the yellow flag. It's just unreal."

At the halfway mark, Fittipaldi, Unser Jr., and Villeneuve were the

Linda McQueeney

only three on the lead lap. Fittipaldi's expensive mistake handed the race to Unser Jr., let Rahal move up to third. As Fittipaldi saw his failed attempt to "hang a lap" on Unser, "My car had slight understeer and that's why I had to come down so low," he explained. "I just tried to go a little lower and hit the apron. I went about a foot too low and hit the corregation (rumble strips) and lost the rear end. I nearly caught it, then the rear end started sliding."

A modest Jacques Villeneuve demurred from any exuberance over his big day. "I didn't see very much of the Penskes and I was just happy to be behind them. I didn't take risks. I just knew I couldn't make a mistake. I just wanted to bring it home. At the same time, I knew I couldn't race the Penskes."

A relieved Rahal was very happy with his third place. "After last year, this is the most wonderful feeling in the world for me and my crew. Our guys worked their butts off to get my car ready. Don't forget that this car was a show car at Penske head-quarters just over a week ago."

STP-backed Jimmy Vasser had the biggest payday of his career for his solid fourth. "I had to tighten my helmet one time when Emerson went by, he went by so hard. We're happy with fourth."

Unser, of course, had the final word. Riding in the pace car after the race with father Al, he noted, "There's Emmo", pointing to the marks on the turn four wall. Father Al opined that, "This place comes back to you." The score for Unser/Fittipaldi showdowns at the speedway now stood at one:one.

Indianapolis 500

Indy 500 photo / Mag Binkley

Indy 500 photo / Linda McQueeney

Ford Motor Company Chairman Alex Trotman and passenger Jay Leno warm up the '95 Mustang Cobra for its pace car duties in front of the 33 car Indianapolis 500 field and an estimated 400,000 spectators, the world's largest single day sports audience.

PENSKES PERFECT IN MILWAUKEE
sweep the top three places

Steve Swope

The quick switch from Indianapolis-dominating Mercedes-Benz power-plants to the Ilmor V8s used on the rest of the PPG Cup circuit, slowed Marlboro Team Penske not at all. Raul Boesel captured the pole, the Penske legions took all three podium positions. Renewing their season long battle of teammates, Al Unser Jr. and Emerson Fittipaldi took down top honors, two laps up on the third Penske standard bearer, Paul Tracy, himself a lap up on the rest of the field. Tracy led the first 22 laps, Fittipaldi the next eight plus seven others. The remaining 155 all fell to the flying Unser. No other driver led even a single lap. Heavy rain forced the race to be red flagged with eight laps to go. It wasn't the first one-two-three sweep for Team Penske. That took place at Michigan in 1980. It was, however, the first time that the Penske team had won four races in a row. Al Jr. pointed out the basis for the Penske sweep. "Handling. At Indianapolis the Mercedes engine was definitely an advantage. But here at Milwaukee, it's the car that's important. The car's got to get through the corner."

"The car was set-up really well," added Unser. "This Marlboro car is a super race car. We've gone from Phoenix to Long Beach to Indy to Milwaukee and the car has been right there at every track."

Fittipaldi also made the point on the Penske's superior handling. "One of the things that happens here is one end of the car is going to give up. You've got to keep the balance here. I could see the other guys fighting with one or the other end of their cars. We worked very hard to try to be consistent, to keep the balance of the car the same throughout the race."

Third place Tracy had no complaints, finishing in the points for the first time in '94. "My car was really good," said Tracy. "We struggled a little bit through the middle of the race. Once Al and Emerson got a lap on me, I had a lap on Mansell, and there was no need to try too hard. I just had to mosey along and finish. It was a good finish for me."

Fourth place fell to Michael Andretti, who passed Mansell on the outside late in the race. "First in class, I guess," said Michael. "I mean, we drove our butt off, and we were lucky to take fourth in the end. But I'll take this fourth. The car wasn't working very well, so I'll take fourth."

Current champion Mansell gave the Penske opposition full marks for their sweep. "What the Penske team demonstrated today was superb. What more can I say?"

Polesitter Boesel had a disappointing outing, finishing eighth with an understeering car. "It was just very bad," said Boesel. "It was very hard to overtake. I had to go inside in three and four over the bumps. I was fighting the push all day long. We just need a lot of development and testing. The Penskes have their act together. Their cars work on rails. They can go in, out, no problem. You start to think they have different tires or something because they're so good."

Unser's third win in a row consolidated his lead in the PPG cup title chase with 79 points, ahead of Fittipaldi with 54, Michael Andretti with 49, and Mansell with 45.

TRACY BUMPS UNSER
scores first 1994 win in ITT Automotive Detroit Grand Prix

Paul Tracy won his first race of the year at the expense of teammate Al Unser Jr., whom he bumped out of the lead, two-thirds of the way through the 77 lap event in Detroit's picturesque Belle Isle Park. Unser was firmly in front on a circuit noted for difficulty in passing. After a restart which positioned Tracy on his tail, Unser had passed a back-marker on the back straight, had two more to go when Tracy punted him. Unser garnered a bent front suspension, soldiered on for a 10th place finish. The third Marlboro Team Penske driver, Emerson Fittipaldi, picked up second place, 16 PPG Cup points, and closed the gap on points leader Unser. Post-race Unser stood at 83 points, while Fittipaldi moved up to 70. Robby Gordon, the Valvoline standard bearer garnered third place in the race, fourth in the points behind Michael Andretti with 59.

Unser passed polesitter Nigel Mansell on the second lap and appeared well on his way to his fourth win in a row, when his day turned bleak. Tracy was apologetic about the circumstances, but not necessarily unhappy with his win. "On the restart, there were a couple of cars that didn't want to let him by," said Tracy. "I'm disappointed to win this way. I'll apologize to Al when I see him. You can't change the result. All I can do is offer an apology. I made a mistake. I was thinking, 'What's Roger going to say?' Clive Howell (Tracy's radio man) said, 'Just settle into a pace and bring it home.' I'm sure I'm going to hear some stuff when I go back to the trailer. But I've never taken anybody out on purpose in my life, and I didn't take Al out."

Unser made no effort to magnify the affair. "Sometimes you eat the bear, and sometimes the bear eats you. Today the bear got us. The good news is we're still in the lead for the championship, ahead of Emerson. Now we just have to concentrate on putting my Marlboro car in victory lane at Portland."

Unser's car ran perfectly until his incident with Tracy. "The car was perfect," said Unser. "I didn't do a thing to my car, didn't change anything, not even a roll bar." The accident left him with a bent front wishbone however. "The steering was cockeyed, and I could see a front A-arm was bent. The tires were flat-spotted as well, and it was shaking so bad my eyeballs were shaking. I could barely see."

Fittipaldi came out the winner in a first half tussle with Mansell. He had pulled away from the current champion when a full course yellow closed up the field. Just after the restart Mansell bumped Fittipaldi, when a slower car in front forced

Steve Swope

Emmo to brake early. Fittipaldi did not indulge in any finger pointing relative to the incident. "It wasn't Nigel's fault. But he did hit me hard, and I was worried that he might have broken my wing mount. I was concerned that the wing would fall off."

Third place Gordon had no regrets. "We're consistently in the top five," said Gordon. "Derrick Walker's giving me a very good car. It's been running flawlessly. The crew was on a par today with Al Jr.'s pit times. You know, we're working hard. We're going to stay up late until we catch up to the Penskes. Maybe we'll have to stay up all night the way they're running."

In view of another Penske one-two finish, which could easily have been one-two-three it may take more than midnight oil to catch the flying Marlboro standard bearers.

The '94 Detroit event was the first organized by International Management Group, which got off to a propitious start, setting new records for attendance and corporate involvement under the direction of Bud Stanner.

Cheryl Day Anderson

Beautiful Belle Isle...ITT Automotive President and CEO Tim Leuliette matches smiles with IMG Chairman Mark McCormack and IMG Motorsports Marketing President Bud Stanner on receiving word that the '94 ITT Automotive Detroit Grand Prix, the first organized by IMG, set new attendance highs.

PENSKE DRIVERS
sweep Portland

Cheryl Day Anderson

Al Unser Jr. won his fourth race of the year and led Marlboro Team Penske to a one-two-three podium sweep in Portland's Budweiser/G.I. Joe's 200. It was the second time this year that the Penske forces had blanketed the top three finishing positions. Not noted for his qualifying talents before joining the Penske operation, Unser was on the pole and led 96 of the race's 102 laps. Fittipaldi, the third fastest qualifier, was in diligent pursuit of Unser almost from the start. He led two laps, finished a close second. Third place Paul Tracy led four laps after starting fourth. None of the other 29 runners even poked a nose into the front spot. Second fastest qualifier Nigel Mansell banged wheels with Tracy as a determined Tracy got by him in the chicane, was pipped for fourth place by Robby Gordon late in the race after he was forced to make a splash-and-go pit stop for fuel.

Unser credited Fittipaldi with applying heavy pressure throughout. "It was almost a panic situation because I could not get Emerson out of my mirrors. I was driving 10/10ths, but I could not do any-

thing to shake Emerson. I couldn't make a single mistake because Emerson would have been on me. So it was a dogfight all the way. I was driving for all I was worth. My biggest moment was that last yellow when Emerson was able to get as close to me as he did."

Fittipaldi, in turn, seemed satisfied with his second place. "I attempted to pass Junior two or three times under braking at the chicane, but I wasn't quite close enough. Two times in traffic Al was slow coming off the last turn, and that helped me get a run at him. But he was braking very deep and I couldn't get beside him. I'm happy," said Fittipaldi, Portland's defending champion. "It was another great race. I was slow on the start, but the last part of the race I was catching Al. He did a fantastic job."

Third place Tracy noted the difficulty of his pass of Mansell. "It was tough to get by Mansell. He had good straightline speed, but he got a little loose coming onto the straightaway, so I was able to get up beside him and outbrake him. He put a squeeze on me and pushed me over onto the grass. I had to bang wheels

to get back onto the track. That was a pretty tough move for both of us."

Gordon who bested Mansell on a last lap dash was happy with his fourth place. "That was one of the best races I've had," said Gordon, who moved into third place in the championship standings although he still seeks his first IndyCar win. "Coming into the last turn I saw it happening. He got right up on somebody, so I laid back and went wide and dove to the inside. He stepped sideways. I stepped sideways and I was able to pull up beside him and just get him at the line. That's what racing's all about. It was a good time."

"I never drove so hard for a fifth place finish," said Mansell. "It was a good, hard race. I held them off as long as I could, but the Penskes are in a different class. I thought I was OK for fourth, but got boxed in."

To top an already glorious day, Unser Jr. claimed the first Marlboro Pole Award bonus of the year, a cool $150,000. Portland was indeed a "happy track" for Unser, who notched his first ever IndyCar victory here a decade ago.

UNSER
takes the Budweiser Grand Prix of Cleveland

When the checkered flag waved at Al Unser Jr. in the Budweiser Grand Prix of Cleveland, the victory score for the season read Marlboro Team Penske, seven, with Unser accounting for five of these; everybody else, one. Current champion Nigel Mansell matched his best result of the year, a solid second place, with Unser teammate Paul Tracy taking third.

"The ball's bouncing my way," said Unser. "What can I say? In racing, one day you're the champ, the next you're the chump. If we rest in any way, shape, or form, we'll be blown off. Our whole goal is to get that number one on the car. In 1985, I had a 36 point lead, and lost the championship to my Dad by one point. So, it ain't over 'til it's over."

Unser overcame a painful back on the bumpy Cleveland airport circuit, finishing ahead of defending PPG Cup champion Nigel Mansell, who tied his best finish of the year. "I was just a little bit sore," said Unser, downplaying his back condition. "That was about it. A lot of people jumped on the back situation thinking I was a little bit weak, but it was OK."

"I drove my ass off," said Mansell, who out-drove Unser's teammate Paul Tracy to second place. "I feel very satisfied. The team did a brilliant job for me. The pit stops were fabulous. I know I drove as hard as I can and we were beaten on the day by a better team, better car, and better driver. That's what this game's all about. We had reliability, so my second place today almost feels like a win."

The defending PPG Cup cham-pion had a couple of incidents during today's race. Once he glanced off the wall coming onto the front straight. He also collided with teammate Mario Andretti, sending Andretti spinning out of the race with a damaged front suspension. "The contact with the wall helped me get around the corner," joked Mansell. "As long as you hit the wall square, it's OK."

Later in the race Mansell found himself being chased hard by Fittipaldi, but a fire in Fittipaldi's engine compartment put an end to his day. "We suspect we had a crack in the headers," said Fittipaldi. "The heat escaped and started the brake lines on fire. Then the bodywork caught on fire. When I went into turn one on that last lap, I had no brakes."

Jacques Villeneuve, leading the

Steve Swope

Rookie of the Year standings, finished fourth. "I didn't like my car at
the beginning of the race," said
Villeneuve. "After we changed tires
at the first pit stop and also made
a rear wing change, the car was a
lot better. I had problems in traffic,
particularly with Robby Gordon running ahead of me. He was one lap
behind, but aggressively racing with
me, and because of that I lost
ground on Tracy."

With the first half of the 16 race
PPG Cup chase complete, Unser
has a generous lead, 127 points to
runner-up Fittipaldi's 86. Current
champion Mansell checks into third
place with 72, followed by Robby
Gordon with 66, Paul Tracy, 64, and
Michael Andretti, 59.

Ron McQueeney

MICHAEL ANDRETTI'S MOLSON INDY TORONTO WIN

his second of the year

Steve Mohlenkamp

Nobody stays on a roll forever; not even Marlboro Team Penske. The vaunted red and white forces faded a bit in the Molson Indy Toronto, after seven victories in a row. The win went to an aggressive Michael Andretti, on the charge all the way from his sixth starting position. Bobby Rahal's crew had his Lola/Honda handling with great precision, enabling him to finish second, his best result of the year and the best ever IndyCar finish for Honda. Even on an off day the Penske forces managed third, with Emerson Fittipaldi, and fifth, with Paul Tracy. Sandwiched between the Marlboro runners was fourth place Mario Andretti in a strong effort.

The race started badly for the favored Penske team when a rare case of engine failure struck Al Unser Jr., the PPG Cup points leader, at the start and he completed only two laps. Early leaders Robby Gordon, the polesitter, and Nigel Mansell, the second fastest qualifier encountered problems, too. Both were afflicted with cut tires, Gordon after leading the first 12

laps, Mansell after leading the next 13. After that it was all Michael except for two Rahal laps in front during the pit stop shuffle. Gordon ended up in sixth place. Mansell eventually dropped out with handling problems.

Michael's trip to the top was not incident free. On the first lap he banged wheels with Tracy and later repeated the process with Mansell. Michael's very durable Reynard survived both collisions without damage, Tracy's Penske and Mansell's Lola were not as fortunate.

Andretti denied any negative intent in the Tracy encounter. "There were a bunch of cars all over the place. I didn't hit Paul on purpose. It was just really tight quarters, and I just clipped him as I went past."

Michael was also able to fight off a late challenge by Rahal. "I knew Bobby was going to be tough today," said Andretti. "I followed him in practice yesterday and his car was working really well."

Andretti credited much of his return to winning form to engineer Morris "Mo" Nunn who returned to

Chip Ganassi's team two weeks earlier. Nunn was with Ganassi in 1992 and 1993, but spent the first half of the '94 season with Dick Simon's team. "I think a lot of it has to do with Mo," said Andretti about today's success. "I believe the combination of Mo and Julian Robertson really works well. We needed somebody to come in from the outside and go through the notes to see things that we might have missed and done wrong. I think Mo's done that for us."

"In the twisty bits, my car was really good," said Rahal, whose previous best finish of the year was third at Indy, albeit without his regular Honda Lola combination. "That's where I was able to beat Emerson today. He was much faster than me down the straight but I could leave him behind in the corners."

In becoming the only driver other than Unser to win more than one race in 1994, Michael consolidated third place in the PPG Cup standings with 80, still well behind Unser with 127 and Fittipaldi with an even 100.

MARLBORO 500
Scott Goodyear survives a race of attrition

The ultra high speed Marlboro 500 is always marked by a high rate of attrition and 1994 was no exception. Only seven cars were circulating at the end and, of those, Scott Goodyear's was circulating the fastest, a full lap ahead of second place Arie Luyendyk with surprise third place runner, Dominic Dobson, another lap behind. The pre-race odds against the trio, or for that matter any one of them, occupying the podium were substantial. Pre-race favorite Nigel Mansell, the '93 winner, nailed down the pole position, aided by the top end advantage of his Ford engine. Ford propelled Raul Boesel and Michael Andretti filled the rest of the three car Ford front row, the first since 1986.

Mansell took off in the lead for 35 very quick laps, gave up on a sticking throttle cable that failed to respond to pit side treatment. "I don't believe it," he said. "I just can't drive it if I can't stop it." That put Michael Andretti out front. He hit the wall on lap 66. Andretti locked up his brakes to avoid a sliding Robby Gordon/ Paul Tracy confrontation, ended up in the wall. After the restart, rookie Jacques Villeneuve nailed the wall in turn three, possibly the result of a cut tire. At the halfway point, the top

four, Boesel, Mario Andretti, Unser Jr., and Fittipaldi were involved in a battle for the lead. Andretti was the first to go—with a blown engine. Boesel and Unser then swapped the top two spots, with Fittipaldi a solid third. When the Penskes pitted, Goodyear, who had been making steady progress, inherited the lead. Not for long. A misreading in the fuel level portion of the engine management system forced him to crawl into the pits with dry tanks. Mauricio Gugelmin then broke a halfshaft, a minor problem compared to Gordon who had a blowout at more than 230 mph and soon after lost an engine.

"Both of those deals were biggies," said Gordon. "You're going at 230 mph and a tire blows out. That's a big one—215 mph and the motor blows up, oils down the rear tires and you slide toward pit lane. The only thing I could think of when I was going there was that I was sideways heading for the pit wall. That kind of scared me, because you've seen so many accidents coming on pit lane wall. So I came off the brakes to get it pointed back and it took off toward the inside wall. I locked 'em up again and I just missed both walls."

All the elements were in place for

an all out fight to the finish among Unser, Boesel, and Fittipaldi. It was not to be. Fittipaldi fell to a broken piston on lap 209. Boesel was next to go with a blown engine.

"We worked on the car every pit stop. It was good in traffic," Boesel said. "I ran a good pace. Little Al put on a little pressure, I respond. It was in the bag. I had to keep the pace I was running to keep ahead of Al. Unfortunately, it wasn't to be, I guess."

Six more laps and it was Al Jr.'s turn to go—another blown engine. "Me and Raul were gonna have a super race," Unser said. "We were pretty even in turns three and four and I could catch him a little bit in one and two. We were just cruising, really. I turned the boost down. There was really no reason for the engine to go."

The lead gravitated back to Goodyear for the second time, with Luyendyk and Dobson who had been making quiet progress slotted in second and third place, one lap and two laps down respectively.

All Goodyear had to do was "cool it", which he did. The win was doubly welcome to the Canadian. He had already been notified that his contract would not be renewed for '95.

MARLBORO TEAM PENSKE
threepeats at Mid-Ohio

Cheryl Day Anderson

For the third time this year, the finely tuned forces of Marlboro Team Penske swept all three podium positions. None of the other 25 drivers in the Miller Genuine Draft 200 at Mid-Ohio was able to lead a single lap. PPG Cup points leader Al Unser Jr. again led the assault, finished on top after a race long duel with teammate Paul Tracy. Again demonstrating his new found qualifying prowess, Unser won the pole position, his fourth of the year, but was cleanly passed by Tracy on the first lap. Tracy led all but one of the first 57 laps, the odd one falling to Emerson Fittipaldi.

Unser was content to let Tracy lead, preferring to wait for the final stages of the race to make his move on first place. Unser never had to attempt the formidable task of getting around Tracy. The lead was handed to him by a stop-and-go penalty assessed on Tracy for passing Robby Gordon on a local yellow flag. "I wasn't planning on passing him," said Tracy about Gordon. "He locked up the brakes and slid wide.

I didn't think it was an issue."

With Tracy's stop-and-go penalty, Unser took the lead. Tracy fell eight seconds behind Unser before a late race full course yellow gave the young Canadian a final chance at beating his teammate. There were two lapped cars between Unser and Tracy for the restart, and Unser was able to build up a cushion before Tracy was able to pass the two slower cars. "I didn't have any close calls today," said Unser. "I needed to finish today, and I didn't take any chances with any lapped cars. Unless it was going to be a solid pass, I didn't do it. Being a little cautious like that helped Paul get away from me a little bit through traffic. I didn't worry too much about it."

"I was on his tail, but passing him would have been something else," said Unser. "We were pretty equal. I could run with him, but I don't know if I had enough car to pass him."

Fittipaldi was third, finishing well behind his two teammates, and the only other car on the lead lap. The 1989 PPG Cup champion joked

about the speed of his younger teammates. "We had a team debriefing this morning," grinned Fittipaldi. "Roger Penske said, 'Take it easy.' But these two guys they were in a rush. They just took off and they're supposed to be taking it easy!"

Robby Gordon finished in fourth place. "It's definitely frustrating," said Gordon. Those Penske cars are working so much better than we are. They're doing something a lot better than we are."

Fifth place went to Michael Andretti who lost time in the pits when an air jack jammed during his first stop. An impressive sixth was Adrian Fernandez. Fernandez beat PPG Cup champion Nigel Mansell by five seconds.

Unser, the leading qualifier of the season, was again the recipient of the Marlboro Pole Award bonus, a $55,000 sweetener to an already happy day; $10,000 for winning the pole, $45,000 in accumulated monies going to the polesitter who also takes the race win.

SLICK 50 200 AT NEW ENGLAND
Penskes prevail again

David Taylor

Another all Marlboro Team Penske winner's podium was the order of the day at the Slick 50 200, the fourth one-two-three sweep of the year for 1994's dominant team. Al Unser Jr. took down his seventh win of the season outdueling teammates Paul Tracy and Emerson Fittipaldi in an exciting battle through heavy traffic in the closing stages. Once again all 24 of the other competitors failed to lead a single lap, including '93 winner and current champion Nigel Mansell, who tried mightily. His strong effort ended dismally at about halfway, when running in second place. In attempting to pass teammate Mario Andretti, who would have been lapped, the two tangled. Andretti went into the wall, Mansell had to give up after a couple of pit stops failed to fix the damage to his car. "My race was going fantastic," said Mansell. "At one point, I thought I was a little bit quicker than the Penskes. Little Al was driving great. But I was just hanging onto him. I was just looking forward to the end of the race."

Tires played an important role in the contest between the Marlboro Team Penske drivers. Fittipaldi blistered his first set of tires, a mistake

that may have cost him the top spot, since he had to make an extra late race fuel stop. "When I blistered the tire in the first segment, I was out of the fuel window," explained Fittipaldi. "I had to make an extra pit stop. The only chance I had was if we would go yellow the last few laps, then I could carry on. But I had no option, I had to come in. When I was driving in the pit road the engine stalled," added Fittipaldi. "That cost me another five seconds there. It's a shame because the car was so hooked today. It was so stable."

Fittipaldi's time in the pits enabled Unser and Tracy to pass their teammate, and the three Marlboro Team Penske cars finished the race in close order, working through traffic as they took the flag.

"I made a couple of tries at Al in traffic," said Tracy. "If it was open road, I don't think I would have gotten by. With the amount of traffic that was in front, I think within a couple of laps, it might have been a good dice."

Accidents eliminated or delayed a handful of top contenders. An accident on the start caused an extended yellow, eliminating Jacques Villeneuve and Arie Luyendyk. Robby Gordon also lost a few laps

in this incident, spinning and stalling On the restart there was another accident, involving Eddie Cheever and Stefan Johansson. A second restart brought together Mike Groff and Scott Sharp with Sharp coming to a stop upside down, but uninjured.

Fourth place went to Dick Simon Racing's Raul Boesel, who qualified on the front row for the fourth time this year, and beat Michael Andretti and Dominic Dobson. Boesel ran with the leaders in the early laps, but fell back battling oversteer. In the closing laps he fought hard, edging Andretti and moving up to eighth in the championship. "We fought a little with Tracy and Emerson in the beginning before I could feel the handling going away," said Boesel. "Over the last 50 laps I had good battle with Michael, but I wish it was for first and second, instead of fourth and fifth."

Al Unser Jr. has a 40 point lead in the PPG Cup point standings after 12 of this year's 16 races. Unser has 173 points followed by Fittipaldi with 133, and Tracy with 107 points. Michael Andretti is fourth in points with 100. Unser could wrap up this year's PPG Cup title early.

AL UNSER JR.
a hero in Molson Indy Vancouver victory

Runner up Robby Gordon almost made it to the winner's circle.

Not even a vicious case of food poisoning could keep Al Unser Jr. out of victory circle in Canada's Molson Indy Vancouver. The debilitating ailment did keep him totally out of Friday's qualifying session. Intravenous fluids were required to get him fit enough to qualify on Saturday, albeit a lowly eighth fastest. Marlboro Team Penske teammates Paul Tracy and Emerson Fittipaldi had pitched in to help set up his car, a favor for which he was duly grateful. Feeling improved but still sub par on raceday, Unser plotted a conservative race strategy, which may not have been a bad idea under the circumstances. There were no less than six full course yellow flags due to accidents or off-course excursions.

Polesitter Robby Gordon took second place, could have been a winner, except for a pair of misfortunes. In one, he suffered a flat tire after being hit from behind by Adrian Fernandez. Next, third gear went away near the end of the race. Michael Andretti overcame the handicaps of two flat tires to finish third. No all Marlboro Team Penske winner's podium this time. Tracy had suspension problems, dropping out after a tangle with Michael Andretti. Fittipaldi was nudged by Nigel Mansell late in the race putting them both out of the race.

Unser readily confessed his conservative stance in the race. "We

watched everyone else run into each other. We were just trying to protect what we had. If anyone stuck their nose in there beside me, it was their corner. Vancouver is a very tough race track, and a tough track to stay out of trouble on. That was our plan today—to stay out of trouble and finish the race."

"I had about 80 percent of my strength back," said Unser. "I wasn't a hundred percent. I felt a hell of a lot better than yesterday. Roger said I even looked better. There was a big difference between today and yesterday. My main objective was to stay anywhere around Emerson and try to finish close to him."

Robby Gordon got off to a flying start before his troubles set in, and even with them, was a fast and determined competitor. He was given full marks by winner Unser. "The main thing on my mind was winning the championship rather than the race. All I can say is thank God Robby lost third gear. Otherwise it would have been tough to hold him off."

"I think I fell to 17th at one point," said Gordon. "It was really frustrating, but I take all the blame. We were getting away from Nigel. Then the caution came out and the pressure was on. He was all over me, the tires were going away and I locked up a tire. I thought that instead of flat spotting a tire, I'd go down the pit lane. But that got me

behind a lot of other guys and we struggled a long time trying to get by people. If you wanted to get by it was almost like you had to hit them."

Michael Andretti was cheered by his third place. "We're into third in the points. We've split the Penskes, so that's good, but it was a tough race. We had two flat tires, and I think at one point we were last. I was driving hard trying to make up time, and we started to have trouble with the rear brakes locking up. I hit a few people because of that, including my father. I apologize to Paul for knocking him out of the race. We hung in there and got some points today, but it's not the way we like to do it."

After the race IndyCar chief steward Wally Dallenbach levied $10,000 fines against both Andretti and Tracy for taking unjustifiable risks and unsportsmanlike driving. Unofficial estimates from the press room had Andretti and Tracy involved in at least half a dozen incidents apiece.

The normally cordial relations between ex-Formula One driving champions Fittipaldi and Mansell cooled considerably after their incident, each blaming the other. Perhaps Mansell summed it up best. "I went down the inside and he had the choice of letting me go or crashing. So, we crashed. I had been pushed-out all day, so I thought I'd give it a go. It was a terrible day out there. The driving was terrible."

VILLENEUVE takes the Texaco-Havoline 200
Unser takes the PPG Cup title

Steve Swope

Sensational Canadian rookie Jacques Villeneuve scored his first IndyCar victory by virtue of a brilliant pass of the Marlboro Team Penske pair of Paul Tracy, the leader, and second place Al Unser Jr. with 15 laps to go. Unser was satisfied with his ultimate second place, which secured him the '94 PPG Cup championship with two races left to run. Tracy, trying desperately to repass Villeneuve, went out with engine failure with seven laps left. The failed engine was a bitter disappointment to the young Canadian, particularly in view of his close race with Michael Andretti for third place in the series.

Winner Villeneuve detailed his virtuoso pass. "I was quicker than them on the straights, but I couldn't get close enough to pass because I would lose downforce when I was behind them. So I was going to go for it on the restart. The fact that Paul made a mistake and got too close to the pace car helped me. He had to back off, and that helped me get the tow."

Villeneuve went for the inside, and was able to pass Tracy as Unser passed on the outside. Tracy momentarily tried to go further inside and hit Villeneuve's left rear tire with his right front wing.

"Paul hit me a little bit in the back," said Villeneuve. "That knocked me sideways, but I was able to get into the corner ahead of them. I knew Paul could afford to make a mistake and go off, but Al couldn't. He had to finish the race to win the championship, so I knew he wouldn't try anything wild. But having him right there behind me all the way to the finish wasn't any fun. It was a lot of pressure."

While Unser nailed down the PPG Cup title and its $1 million award, Villeneuve put the Rookie of the Year title, worth $50,000, on ice and gave clear indication of bigger things to come.

Emerson Fittipaldi came all the way from ninth on the starting grid to finish third, at no time a threat to teammate Unser ahead of him. The always gracious Fittipaldi complimented both Villeneuve and new champion Unser. "He did a fantastic job," said Fittipaldi of Villeneuve. "The last 10 laps with all the pressure from Al and me, he never made a mistake. He showed a lot of maturity just like at Indianapolis." On teammate Unser, "Al Jr. has done a great job for Marlboro Team Penske, and I know he will be a great champion and ambassador for our sport."

Teo Fabi finished fourth, equalling his best finish of the year for Jim Hall's team. Fabi picked up places on both of his pit stops, beating home Adrian Fernandez and Raul Boesel. Fernandez scored the best result of his IndyCar career after running strongly throughout the race.

Among those failing to finish the Texaco-Havoline 200 were Mario and Michael Andretti both of whom suffered engine failures and Robby Gordon who was an early retirement from the race with a broken transmission.

The '93 PPG Cup champion, Nigel Mansell, went quietly with a misfiring engine and a non-points paying finish.

TRACY ON TOP
in another Marlboro Team Penske sweep

Steve Swope

It was Paul Tracy's turn to lead the Marlboro Team Penske threesome to the winner's podium, their fifth one-two-three sweep of the season. Once again, none of the 23 other competitors managed a lap in the lead. Long overdue for an oval track victory, Tracy made no mistakes this time, leading 192 laps of the 200 total, with five going to Al Unser Jr. and three to Emerson Fittipaldi. The fourth place runner, Raul Boesel, was four full laps in arrears at the end.

Winner Tracy supplied the details on his welcome and long awaited oval track win. "I said I was going to let Emerson go at the start, but my car was working great on the outside. I was able to run high without any trouble, so I went for it and took the lead. My car got a little bit loose in packs of traffic. I don't think my car was as good as Al's in traffic, but it was great in clean air. My crew did a great job in the pits as well. They got me out fast without any problems every time."

Tracy pointed out how difficult it is to win on an oval. "These ovals are

really, really tough to win on," he said. "A lot of it is strategy and a lot of it is set-up. I've been competitive, especially on the short ovals, but you've got to get everything right to win. Today I was thinking about changing the car during the race because I had a lot of understeer. I talked to Rick Mears on the radio and decided not to touch it."

New champion Unser, who needs only 10 points in the year's final race at Laguna Seca to set a modern scoring record, was generous in his praise of Marlboro Team Penske. "I've always said our cars shine on race day, and today, our cars were head and feet above any other car out there. I congratulate (chief designer) Nigel Bennett and all the people in England who build our cars. When all three of us got to racing here we left 'em in the dust."

Unser also made the point that the Penske drivers put every effort into avoiding any problems with their cars getting too tail-happy in the race. This is a common handling problem at Nazareth, and seems to have been even more of a problem

this year with smaller wings mandated on short ovals and road courses than last year.

Fittipaldi noted some problems with traffic. "I got stuck in traffic a few times. I had some bad luck with traffic, and couldn't get through it as quick as I should have. But I was very pleased with my car's handling. We didn't have anything like the problems we had last year."

The best of the non-Penskes, Boesel, was happy with his fourth place. "We put a lap on every car in the field other than the Penskes. We couldn't keep up with them, but it was a good race for us, considering. My car was quite neutral except for when I got behind people. Then it got loose."

Fifth place went to Johansson who finished one lap ahead of Teo Fabi and one more lap ahead of Road America's winner, Jacques Villeneuve. Johansson recovered from a stop-and-go penalty for using the warm up lane under a yellow flag. He said his car was a little loose, but nowhere as bad as most others.

PAUL TRACY
takes Toyota Grand Prix of Monterey

The season finale belonged to a brilliant Paul Tracy who left Marlboro Team Penske on a high note. The young Canadian who will move to Newman/Haas Racing in 1995 to partner Michael Andretti, won the pole and led all of the 84 laps around the beautiful Laguna Seca circuit. Nobody, including teammates Al Unser Jr., the new PPG Cup champion and series runner-up Emerson Fittipaldi, put any serious pressure on the flying Tracy who finished with a 21.417 second cushion. Raul Boesel, up from eighth on the starting grid, finished second in his last drive for the Dick Simon team. He's going to Rahal/Hogan Racing in '95. Second qualifier Jacques Villeneuve filled the third place on the winner's podium. In *his* last Indy-Car drive, celebrated veteran Mario Andretti, who leads the all-time IndyCar statistics in starts (407), laps led (7587), and poles (66), bowed out with engine failure while running in a strong second place. He was the guest of honor at a string of celebrations over the weekend.

At one point in today's race, the Penske team was running one-two-three, but the PPG Cup champion, Al Unser Jr., failed to finish because of transmission failure, while Fittipaldi was shouldered back to fourth place by Boesel and Villeneuve. Tracy's victory was the 12th of the season for Marlboro Team Penske, a new record for a team in IndyCar racing.

Fifth and sixth today were taken by Teo Fabi and Arie Luyendyk.

One measure of Marlboro Team Penske's strength was the remarkable total of 1584 laps led of 2083 completed during the year. In essence, more than two-thirds of the time throughout the entire season, a Marlboro Team Penske driver was out in front. While the statistics don't show it, chances are a second red and white car was right behind the front runner.

Brian Leshon

TECHNOLOGY
Penske leads the pack

By Arthur M. Flax

Technology buffs started 1994 with high hopes that the many manufacturers in IndyCar racing—Penske, Reynard, Lola, Ilmor, Ford-Cosworth, and Honda—would provide plenty of variety in the winner's circle and some close contests for series honors. The superb Penske chassis, powered by Ilmor engines with new found power, dashed those hopes. The hint of things to come lay in Paul Tracy's runaway victory for Penske in the last race of 1993.

Even within Penske's record breaking sweep there were points of technical interest, the most startling of which was the Mercedes-Benz Indy 500 engine. There was no question that a large, turbocharged pushrod engine built to long standing Indy 500 rules could deliver more power than the industry standard double overhead cam IndyCar engines produced by Cosworth and Ilmor. But it seemed unlikely that a manufacturer with the resources to develop a reliable pushrod Indy 500 engine would take the considerable financial and public relations risk. Ilmor's all new Indy 500 winning Mercedes-Benz engine, built in near total secrecy over the course of several months, clearly displayed the firm's talent in racing engine design and manufacturing technology. The project also demonstrated the Penske/Mercedes-Benz alliance's willingness to take a big risk and share the substantial rewards of success. The Mercedes-Benz Indy 500 engine was clearly the top technical news of the year.

The engine likely produced in the range of 1,000 horsepower, taking advantage of Indianapolis only rules that allowed a larger, purpose-built, two valve per cylinder pushrod engine to compete against smaller, four valve per cylinder racing engines. Ilmor started the Mercedes-Benz project in October 1993 and ran the first engine in February, a remarkably short time from drawing board to test bed.

For 10 years, Buick had tried to win Indy with a pushrod engine, finishing as high as third in 1993 with driver Al Unser Sr. Unfortunately, Buick's V6 engine started life as a production powerplant with all the inherent disadvantages of production based design. The Mercedes-Benz 500I (as the engine

was named) was a different animal, a pure racing engine, designed from the outset to last the 500 mile race. In light of that, it was interesting to listen to the Mercedes on the Indianapolis track. The big engine sounded smooth and powerful and relatively unstressed. By comparison, Buick Indy engines typically emitted a characteristic roar implying a highly stressed powerplant. Not that sound is a substitute for test bed measurements, but it is a psychological yardstick.

The Mercedes-Benz 500I displaced 3.43 liters and was turbocharged to 55 inches (1.86 times atmospheric pressure) boost. By comparison, the Ilmor Indy V8D and Ford-Cosworth XB, double overhead cam racing engines, are limited to 2.65 liters and 45 inches of boost.

Placing a different engine into an Indy car specifically designed for another engine can create handling problems. Some experts (and wags) thought the high powered Penske cars were actually sandbagging during qualifying.

But Penske engineer John Faivre said, "The Mercedes-Benz 500I had so much power, it actually contributed to handling problems. There was so much more acceleration and deceleration on the Speedway. Typically an Indy car (on the Indianapolis Motor Speedway) will operate in the 220 to 235 mph speed range. Our car operated from 220 to 245 mph."

Accelerative forces transfer weight between the back and front wheels. Under deceleration, more weight is distributed to the front wheels and the rear end becomes lighter—one reason why it is so important for a racing driver to smoothly transition on or off the throttle.

In order to improve the handling of the Mercedes-Benz powered Penske at Indianapolis, Faivre said, "More downforce was added."

Driver Emerson Fittipaldi noted, "The extra power allowed us to use added downforce. That made the car more stable and easier to drive."

Faivre pointed out a negative aspect of this move. "With the added downforce, the pole and race winning car didn't go as fast as we thought it would."

In addition to the handling adjustments, the Penske/Mercedes-Benz was

fitted with a special gearbox to cope with the added power. As for its effect on the packaging and weight distribution of the Penske, Faivre said the Mercedes was actually lighter than the Ilmor V8D, due to its simpler design.

"Ilmor had planned to build the 209 (as it is called inside the company) for 1995, but as a result of rules changes penalizing the pushrod design, the company decided the engine would have been uncompetitive without further development," said Paul Ray, vice president of engineering for the Ilmor Engineering Inc. division in Detroit.

Except for the advent of the Mercedes-Benz powerplant, the Ilmor Indy V8D which powered Penske cars to their 11 other victories would have been a top story. The V8D provided yet another example of Ilmor's ability to introduce all new engines at a moment's notice.

The V8D was not an updated version of the Indy V8C, but an all new engine with a different V angle (approximately 85 degrees versus 80 degrees in the C). The D also featured a shorter stroke for higher revs, a revised cylinder head port shape, and different manifold. Delco electronics, used in the earlier engines, were retained. Ray said, "The new engine developed over 800 horsepower at more than 13,000 rpm."

For customers, Ilmor also introduced an updated version of the Indy V8C, called the C+, during 1994.

Did the Indy V8D produce more power than the Ford-Cosworth XB? Hard to say. At Michigan, a "horsepower" track, the Cosworth was clearly faster during qualifying. But Penske's competition said the D seemed to produce good mid-range horsepower, used to advantage in the superb Penske chassis on road courses and shorter tracks.

Penske competitors put it this way, "Our perception was not that they had so much horsepower, but the ability to put the horsepower down." This speaks well for the Penske/Ilmor package.

Ford-Cosworth XB, the top engine of 1993, remained a potent powerplant during 1994, with some very progressive technical updates.

Steve Miller, chief engineer, IndyCar program for Cosworth, said, "On super-speedways, the XB still demonstrated

Our Name Says It All!

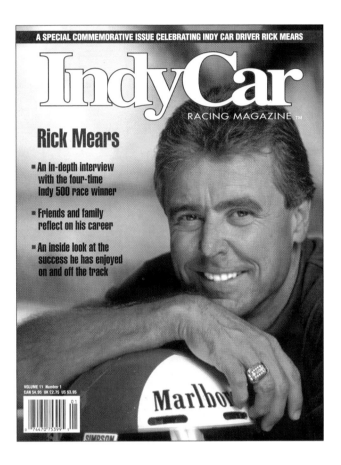

a conclusive edge. In fact, Michael Andretti, who will drive for Newman/Haas in '95, recently tested at 230 mph at Indianapolis in a 1994 Lola with XB power. But the Ilmor powered Penske was a superior package on road circuits." How much of that superiority was due to the engine and how much to the chassis is not clear.

Miller said, "The combination of our engine and the Lola was not as competitive as we would have liked it to be. Whether the gap between the Ilmor and the Cosworth narrowed in '94 is difficult to say."

The 1994 Ford-Cosworth XB retained its 80 degree V8 layout and produced, according to Miller, over 800 horsepower. "The engine," he said, "produced peak horsepower at 12,500 rpm, but engines typically revved over 13,000 rpm. Power has been improved on an average of four percent per year, over the three years the engine has raced."

Among the changes for 1994 Miller said, "The biggest was our ABC control. That stands for Automatic Boost Control. In previous engines, the ninth butterfly at the plenum inlet was controlled mechanically. We separated that control (from the other throttle butterflies) and installed an electric motor. Calibrated with the waste gate, that allowed for precise tuning. The electronics then allowed us to get all the permissible boost. This is important since you get fluctuations in boost during transitions on or off the throttle.

Essentially, ABC allowed Cosworth engines to get more power, more of the time.

The third powerplant of significance in 1994 was the Honda Indy V8. Honda sent shock waves through the Indy car ranks when it entered IndyCar racing in '94 after an intensive testing cycle in '93. Honda had a sparkling record in Formula One, before it abandoned that field for the IndyCar arena.

Almost unbelievably, Honda was off the mark in its first year of IndyCar racing. Off to a slow start, Bobby Rahal's Honda powered car failed to qualify for the Indy 500. Rahal bailed out at the last minute, qualified a rented year old Penske with Ilmor D power. Starting back in the pack, he finished third, proving that the driver was not the missing ingredient.

Honda describes the engine as a 750+ horsepower, double overhead cam V8 with Honda electronic fuel injection and Honda/Motorola electronic engine management.

The engine was rumored to weigh 100 pounds more than the Ilmor. In addition to the weight problem, the engine had a spotty reliability record.

Another rumor, that Honda engineers tried a crankshaft design where two pistons fired at once, was said to be unfounded. Honda had used a similar

scheme in motorcycle racing to improve traction with its powerful engines. However, all manner of crankshaft designs were tried.

Despite the lack of success in its first season, it would be foolish to count Honda out in the IndyCar arena. The company has a record of technical brilliance and a history of perseverance.

On the chassis front, chalk up another stellar performance by Penske designers and engineers. The '94 edition simply outhandled the competition, was noted for superb balance, the ability to maintain adhesion under full or near-empty fuel loads.

When Paul Tracy ran away from the field at Laguna Seca in the last race of the 1993 season, his victory foreshadowed the events of the following season. According to Penske electronics engineer, John Faivre, Tracy's convincing win, "had to do with a substantive power gain." In fact, claimed Faivre, "The biggest single change from the start of 1993 to the start of '94 was in horsepower." But the Penske chassis deserves full marks for its ability to use the extra horsepower.

"Improved aerodynamics also played a part in the Penske success," he said. The most apparent aerodynamic feature of the car was its oft copied rear fin.

Emerson Fittipaldi said of the fin, "We tested it at Phoenix in the winter. It provided cleaner air to the rear wing and more downforce."

Peter Gibbons, Newman/Haas engineer said, "The fin added weight, but didn't affect performance."

Gibbons credited the Penske cars with having a superior combination of aerodynamics and a very tractable engine on road courses. He also praised the team's three superb drivers for their ability to develop the cars at an exceptional rate. In terms of test driver hours available, three adds up to 50% more than two.

On top in '93, new for 1994, the Lola T94/00 was fast during qualifying, but performance often fell off the pace as the race progressed. Despite six pole positions, its only win came at the hands of Scott Goodyear at the Michigan 500. Although Goodyear's win was largely due to attrition, Raul Boesel, in another Lola/Ford-Cosworth XB, led most laps in the race.

The T94/00 represented Lola's first use of an all carbon fiber IndyCar tub. Previous Lola Indy cars had retained (increasingly smaller as the design progressed) aluminum sections behind the front wheels.

The major change in the Lola for 1994 came at the rear, where a sequentially shifted transverse gearbox was incorporated.

According to Newman/Haas engineer, Peter Gibbons, "The transverse gearbox made a big difference in polar moment of inertia, and allowed for a bigger dif-

fuser to increase downforce."

In other words, the shorter gearbox eliminated a large amount of weight, hanging behind the rear wheels, and greater airflow through the ground effects tunnels under the car.

As the season progressed, Newman/Haas, considered the factory Lola team, tried to improve downforce with less drag—considered by many engineers to be a major advantage of the Penske chassis.

Of these continuous efforts for improvement, Gibbons said, "We produced a better road course wing for Detroit." Driver Nigel Mansell got the Detroit pole, one of three for the year.

When Michael Andretti won in Australia driving the never before raced Reynard 94I, hopes were high that the new car would give the Penskes a run for their money. Not only did the car win its first race, but it demonstrated its extreme ruggedness, shrugging off Andretti's spirited curb bouncing. The Reynard won two more times, once again with Andretti at Toronto and again with Jacques Villeneuve at Elkhart Lake. The young Canadian, a star in his rookie year, also ran strongly at Indianapolis, finishing second, at Laguna Seca (third), and Cleveland (fourth).

Designed by Malcolm Oastler, the Reynard was distinguishable from its competitors by its delta wing design and relatively high nose. The car featured, as is characteristic IndyCar practice, front and rear pushrod suspension. It was, however, the only Indy car to feature a longitudinal gearbox. Reynard tested with a shorter longitudinal gearbox at Laguna Seca late in the year and reports are that the smaller, lighter gearbox will be incorporated on the 1995 model.

The chassis scorecard for 1994 tells a stark tale of Penske superiority. Penske 12 wins, 10 poles; Reynard 3 wins, no poles; and Lola 1 win, 6 poles.

Continuing a program started in 1993, General Motors placed "crash recorders" in every car during every race. The recorders sample G loads in three planes 2,000 times per second, up to 200 Gs.

John Melvin, senior staff research engineer in the GM Research and Development Center, said, "This year we got 47 important readings from 84 incidents. There were (thankfully) few frontal impacts, but at Indianapolis, Stan Fox pulled 60 Gs in a crash with only minor injuries."

More important than anecdotal demonstrations of human endurance, Fox's crash again demonstrated that the changes which made Indy cars stiffer—transferring more shock to the driver's body, but providing for less intrusion into the cockpit—made them safer. The nose cone on Fox's car crushed symmetrically and completely, but his legs were not severely injured.

Bob Steig

A FORD FAREWELL TO THREE OF INDYCAR'S GREATEST DRIVERS

You won't be seeing Mario Andretti, Al Unser, or Johnny Rutherford in Indy cars in '95. All three announced their retirement from active IndyCar driving in '94. Among them they have 118 IndyCar victories, 8 IndyCar Driver's Championships, and 8 Indianapolis 500 wins, many of these in Ford powered cars. They'll still be driving however. In appreciation of their accomplishments, Ford Division General Manager and Ford Motor Co. Vice President Ross Roberts, shown at the Detroit Grand Prix, presented each with a new Ford Mustang Cobra, similar to the Mustangs which served as the race's pace cars.

Steve Swope

Jimmy Vasser, one of the young lions gaining increased attention on the IndyCar circuit, has a new home at Chip Ganassi Racing and a new Target/STP Reynard Ford in which to hunt down his first victory in the PPG Cup series.

Motorsports Marketing
at a
Championship Level

Indy Car Australia
March 16-19

ITT Automotive Detroit Grand Prix
June 9-11

Medic Drug Grand Prix of Cleveland
Presented By Dairy Mart
July 21-23

Grand Prix of Dallas
September 8-10

We'll See You At The Track In '95

For More Information Contact:

IMG *Motorsports*
One Erieview Plaza, Suite 1300
Cleveland, Ohio 44114
(216) 522-1200

DRIVERS

Dale Earnhardt captures a landmark seventh title

By Tom Higgins

The 1994 NASCAR Winston Cup Series season will be remembered both for numbing tragedy and towering triumph.

It started with drivers Neil Bonnett and Rodney Orr losing their lives 72 hours apart in separate, single car accidents while practicing for the Daytona 500 in February. The title chase ended early with Earnhardt holding an unassailable lead with two races to go.

Career threatening injuries to superstar Ernie Irvan and former Busch Series Grand National champion Chuck Bown added to the season-long anguish. These tragedies tempered but could not extinguish the excitement generated by Dale Earnhardt's unstoppable drive to a seventh Winston Cup championship, tying the once seemingly invincible record of retiree Richard Petty.

Though deeply saddened by the death of Bonnett, his best friend, Earnhardt opened the season in his now standard role as an overwhelming favorite to win the Daytona 500 for the first time in 16 years of trying. Typically, the driver nicknamed "The Intimidator" drove awesomely in the preliminaries at Daytona International Speedway.

He qualified second fastest for the classic in the Richard Childress Racing team's black no. 3 Chevrolet, missing the pole by .031 seconds as Ford driver Loy Allen became the first rookie to top time trials for the 500. Earnhardt then won, in order, the Busch Clash special event matching the previous season's pole winners, a Gatorade Twin 125-mile qualifying race leading to the 500, and the Goody's 300 for Grand National cars.

The latter was his fifth straight triumph in the 300-miler that traditionally opens the Busch Series tour.

Expectedly, Earnhardt went to the front in the 500 and he had his Chevy in the lead 10 times for 45 laps. But unexpectedly the car wasn't handling as well as earlier in the week. During the race's waning stages Earnhardt started

slipping back, despite his skilled and unflagging efforts.

At the end, he wound up seventh on the lead lap, watching Sterling Marlin, driving the Morgan/McClure team's Chevrolet, outduel Ford ace Irvan for the victory. It was Marlin's first Winston Cup triumph in 279 starts.

As deeply disappointed as Earnhardt was at being denied once more in the Daytona 500, he expressed happiness for the likable Marlin, who notched his first victory in the "Big One".

Earnhardt, seeking that seventh title, finished seventh again in the season's second race, the Goodwrench 500 at North Carolina Motor Speedway. This result produced the predictable number of witty remarks from wags in the press corps, which Earnhardt took no more seriously than their effusive praise when he was winning.

"The Intimidator" moved up to fourth place in Richmond's Pontiac 400, finishing on the lead lap with winner Irvan. Problems traced to "Tire War II" between incumbent Goodyear and challenger Hoosier left Earnhardt 12th, three laps down, the following week in the Purolator 500 at Atlanta.

Many NASCAR observers feel Earnhardt is at his best on the demanding 1.366-mile, egg-shaped Darlington track. He reinforced that thinking by taking the TranSouth 400, a race that since 1973 had been 100 miles longer. The victory snapped a 17-race non-winning streak and gave Earnhardt 60 career triumphs, sixth on the all-time list.

Earnhardt won again the following week at the bowl-like Bristol Raceway in Tennessee, scoring his first short track victory since early October of 1991. That performance moved Earnhardt into first place in the standings, 40 points ahead of Irvan. He would hold either first or second place the rest of the 31 race season.

Solid finishes of fifth and 11th followed on the short tracks at North Wilkesboro and Martinsville, VA. Irvan took the latter

show to regain the point standings lead.

The Winston Select 500 at Talladega (AL) Superspeedway, NASCAR's fastest track, was billed as an Earnhardt/Irvan showdown. The two didn't disappoint approximately 150,000 fans and a national television audience on May 1. Wildly scrubbing sheet metal as if they were racing on the dirt short track just up the road, the two hurtled toward the checkered flag. Earnhardt got there first, sweeping under the flagstand a scant .06 seconds ahead of Irvan's Ford.

Earnhardt voiced optimism about a first road course victory the following Sunday at Sears Point after qualifying fourth. He ran well, but Irvan, driving before a partisan California crowd in his home state proved unbeatable. Earnhardt, nonetheless, had his best showing at the track near the Sonoma Valley, placing third.

Back home in North Carolina at Charlotte Motor Speedway for the Coca-Cola 600 on Memorial Day weekend, Earnhardt and his Childress teammates once again were optimistic. They had a new car for the 400-lap day-into-night marathon at the sport's only lighted superspeedway. The sleek Lumina had run extremely well in open testing leading to NASCAR's longest race. However, problems developed. Earnhardt managed to qualify only 24th fastest. He made a charge toward the front, but the problems returned, and he fell back, losing three laps. Attrition among other drivers enabled Earnhardt to finish ninth and maintain second place in the points chase. More misfortune awaited the next weekend at Dover Downs, the Monster Mile in Delaware.

An early tire problem cost Earnhardt a lap, which he courageously made up with a stirring charge, although tires of others continued to pop all the way around the track. On lap 288, Earnhardt was involved in a crash, heavily damaging his Chevy. After 75 laps in the garage for repairs, he returned to take 28th place, good enough to keep him second in the point standings.

The next five races produced a stretch of splendid showings that swept Earnhardt back atop the point standings and heightened anticipation that he really *was* enroute to matching Petty's remarkable record.

Earnhardt placed second, second, third, and second in the summer events at Pocono, Michigan, Daytona, and New Hampshire, respectively. The Pepsi 400 at Daytona yielded Earnhardt's first pole of the '94 campaign.

Back at the triangular Pocono track in Pennsylvania for the fifth race in the stretch, Earnhardt finished seventh. In that string of races Earnhardt finished every lap of a possible 1060.

He was rolling.

When Earnhardt won the pole for the season's second race at Talladega, rivals sighed. Normally when he starts at the front on the sprawling 2.66-mile Alabama speedway there's no catching him. However, this time Earnhardt experienced a rare engine failure on the 80th of the race's 188 laps and he parked, to finish 34th. This gave the standings lead back to Irvan.

A sizzling run by Rick Mast in a Ford denied Earnhardt the pole for the inaugural Brickyard 400, a starting spot he openly craved. Mast guessed that to make up for the disappointment, Earnhardt would go all out to lead the first lap.

Earnhardt did, and scraped the turn four wall, damaging his car's right front. Earnhardt pitted several times for repairs, dropping back to 38th place but remaining on the lead lap. He rallied impressively to finish fifth and regain the points lead for good. Rival Irvan was victimized by a cut tire late in the race while battling for the lead.

Earnhardt then made it a sweep of the "show" positions in the series' two road course races, finishing third at Watkins Glen, NY, the same spot he claimed in the spring at Sears Point.

On a soft, warm Saturday morning in the Irish Hills of Michigan, another heart stopping accident occurred, one that shook stock car racing almost as much as the deaths of Bonnett and Orr and the loss of superstars Alan Kulwicki and Davey Allison in aviation accidents the year before. During practice for the GM Goodwrench 400, Ernie Irvan's Ford smashed fullbore into the turn two wall at Michigan International Speedway. The popular driver incurred life-threatening injuries to the head and lungs. Few competitors had much heart for racing the next day, and Earnhardt didn't have to run far. He crashed on lap 54 while attempting to pass Todd Bodine in turn three. He had no choice but to park, finishing 37th. Earnhardt's lead jumped to 79 points over an unlucky Irvan who was out for the season. Frontrunner Earnhardt now led Mark Martin by a commanding 206 points and Rusty Wallace by 213 as they became the top challengers to chase him through the final 10 races.

Earnhardt then unwrapped his second incredible streak of the season, a sizzling stretch drive that wrapped up the record-tying seventh title for the second generation driver from Kannapolis, NC.

His next eight races produced these finishes: Goody's 500, Bristol, third; Southern 500, Darlington, second; Miller 400, Richmond, third; Splitfire 500, Dover, second; Goody's 500, Martinsville, second; Holly Farms 400, North Wilkesboro, seventh; Mello Yello 500, Charlotte, third; and AC Delco 500, North Carolina Motor Speedway, first.

Earnhardt's fourth victory of 1994 left him an unbeatable 448 points ahead of Wallace, with races remaining at Phoenix and Atlanta.

To take the record-tying title in winning style, Earnhardt had to hold off a fast-closing Mast in a thriller, taking the checkered flag by about a half-car length.

The champion's worst finish of the season ensued at Phoenix as he placed 40th, sidelined by engine failure. He rebounded to finish second at Atlanta, closing the season positively after twice making up a lap lost to tire problems.

Earnhardt finished with 20 top five finishes and 25 top 10s for earnings of $3,300,733, including a $1.25 million championship prize from R.J. Reynolds Tobacco Co. The purse pushed his career total to $22,914,304, a record for all of motorsports.

It took almost a month for the scope of the accomplishment, matching King Richard's once seemingly invincible mark, to sink in on Earnhardt, now a resident of Mooresville, NC.

Mark Martin outdueled fellow Ford driver Rusty Wallace for second place in the point standings although beaten for race victories, 8-2.

Martin and his Jack Roush Racing team appeared to have shaken the slow starts that have plagued the operation for years. After finishing 13th in the season-opening Daytona 500, Martin recovered to showings of fourth, sixth, fifth, and second in the next four races.

However, five of the next seven events found Martin finishing 21st, 13th, 38th, 16th, and 32nd before there was a rally for five straight top five showings.

Finally, the breakthrough to victory lane came in the 20th race of the season on the road course at Watkins Glen, where Martin started a four-race winning tear in 1993. The unassuming Martin simply overwhelmed his opposition, starting from the pole and leading 75 of the Bud at the Glen's 90 laps. He only surrendered the lead in the pit stop shuffle.

Martin's other triumph came in the season finale Hooters 500 at Atlanta Motor Speedway. Combined with Wallace's 32nd place finish, which resulted from a hole in the oil pan caused by debris from a wreck, the victory gave Martin the runnerup position in the point standings. Martin's 43 point edge over Wallace meant an extra $115,000 in his post-season bonus check of $350,000.

Martin appeared headed to several other wins, most notably at Darlington and Dover in September. However, engine failure in the waning laps struck at Darlington and a cut tire, resulting from a collision while lapping Ricky Rudd, victimized Martin at Dover.

Wallace quickly answered one of the 1993-94 off-season's most intriguing questions: Would a switch from Pontiac, with which his Penske South Team had won 10 races in 1993, to the Ford Thunderbird troupe handicap Wallace in 1994? It took Wallace only two races to prove the answer. No!

The bad luck that has hounded Wallace at Daytona for years was evident again in the 500 as he was swept into a wreck not of his making on the 61st of the race's 200 laps, finishing 41st.

But he won the very next Sunday at Rockingham, scoring at the speedway in the North Carolina Sandhills for a third straight time and fifth overall.

Wallace won again at Martinsville in late April, taking a Hanes 500 thriller over Irvan. He then "swept" June, winning all three of the month's races at Dover, Pocono, and Michigan.

Wallace scored a stirring victory by a scant .16 seconds over Martin at Bristol in August, evading a rash of wrecks under the track's lights before a crowd of almost 70,000. Back-to-back victories at Dover and Martinsville in September for a season sweep of those tracks kept Wallace hopeful of a whirlwind finish that would provide his second season long championship.

It wasn't to be. A timing chain failure doomed Wallace to a 37th place finish in the Mello Yello 500 at Charlotte and when engine problems dropped him to a lowly 35th place finish at Rockingham, Earnhardt administered the coup de grace by winning.

Irvan, starting his first full season with Robert Yates Racing, took two of the first four, whipping to victories in March at Richmond and Atlanta, tracks he never conquered before. A virtually flawless performance added a third victory at Sears Point.

Along the way there were six "close misses", runnerup finishes at Daytona in February, at Martinsville and Talladega in the spring, at Dover, Daytona, and Watkins Glen during the summer.

Then came that awful Saturday at the Michigan track and, with it, the injuries that sidelined Irvan for the season and left the future of his driving career uncertain. Irvan was only 27 points behind Earnhardt in the title race when he was hurt, listing 13 top five finishes and 15 top 10s in 20 races.

Terry Labonte and Geoff Bodine also won three times each.

Labonte triumphed in the First Union 400 at North Wilkesboro in April, ending a non-winning streak of 135 races dating to July of 1989. Labonte, who had joined the Hendrick Motorsports Chevrolet team at the start of the season, posted only mediocre results through the rest of the spring and summer before winning again at Richmond in September and at Phoenix on Halloween weekend.

Labonte was in front the last 18 laps in his victory at North Wilkesboro, but dominated at Richmond, setting the pace for 237 of 400 laps. He was ahead 112 of 312 laps in a Phoenix shootout with Martin.

Labonte placed seventh in points, flashing the form that brought him the 1984 championship.

Bodine, who provided the flagship team for Hoosier's effort, in a return to Winston Cup competition for the first time since 1989, sparkled with a victory in the Winston Select all-star race at Charlotte in May. He got his first points race victory as a Winston Cup team owner by outrunning fellow Hoosier-users Ward Burton, Joe Nemechek, and Jeff Burton at Pocono in July.

Bodine added a big victory at Michigan in August and he won again at North Wilkesboro in October, finishing a whopping 21 seconds ahead of runnerup Labonte.

Tempering Bodine's five pole, three win season were a rash of costly accidents and engine failures, plus a much lamented tangle in the inaugural Brickyard 400 at Indianapolis Motor Speedway with his brother, Brett. The two exchanged bumps at the front of the field, and Geoff spun. He crashed while leading, later revealed a "family feud" that had been unknown to all but a few in the Winston Cup garage area.

Youthful Jeff Gordon and take-no-prisoners charger Jimmy Spencer dashed onto the Winston Cup winners' list with a pair of victories, each in spectacular fashion.

Gordon, driving a Chevy for Hendrick Motorsports, captured the best 600-miler at Charlotte since the Benny Parsons/Darrell Waltrip duel in 1980. After battling with Rusty Wallace and Geoff Bodine throughout, Gordon's chances hinged on a final green flag pit stop. Both his older rivals had opted to take on four tires, so Gordon and his crew chief, Ray Evernham, gambled on a two-tire stop. The strategy put the 22 year old Gordon in front and he stayed there for a first victory that left him happy but tearful in victory lane.

After a stirring door-to-door duel with Irvan in the biggest NASCAR happening in years, the Brickyard 400 at Indianapolis Motor Speedway, Gordon prevailed after his rival cut a tire with five laps to go. It

was a storybook, back-home-again-in-Indiana triumph for a youngster who grew up only a few miles from the historic track.

Gordon took eighth place in the points race. No one ever questioned Spencer's courage or his hearty right foot in a race car. How effectively he used his brain while on the track was a question often raised by insiders.

Spencer revved both up at the same time in the Pepsi 400 and made a last lap pass of the savvy Irvan to win at Daytona. Sparks flew off the sheet metal of both cars. The only lap Spencer led during the race was the final one, as he won for the first time in 130 starts.

Spencer put the same Ford fielded by the Junior Johnson team in the winner's circle in Talladega's DieHard 500 two weeks later, holding off nominal teammate Bill Elliott in the final frantic laps.

Scoring one victory each were Sterling Marlin, Ricky Rudd, Elliott, and Dale Jarrett.

By far the biggest triumph, and longest overdue, was that of Marlin, who took the Daytona 500 in his first start for the Morgan/McClure team. In 279 previous races dating to 1978, the second generation driver, son of colorful Clifton "Coo Coo" Marlin, never had been to a Winston Cup victory lane.

After sparkling work in the pits gave Sterling's Chevy a handling edge, he came on at the end to outrun Irvan in a thriller and score the most popular triumph in years. As Marlin coasted down pit road after winning, members of every team walked out to shake his hand or offer a high five.

Ricky Rudd realized what seemed an unlikely goal at the start of the season, a victory in his first year as a team owner, starting from scratch. That win came in the Slick 50 300 at New Hampshire. Irvan had the strongest car and dominated most of the race, leading 176 laps. However, Irvan and Geoff Bodine tangled with 20 laps to go on the slick racing surface, both crashing.

This left it to Rudd and Earnhardt to settle a Ford/Chevy shootout. Rudd grabbed the lead in the last eight miles to beat a fierce rival by about five car lengths.

Rudd had said a top 10 finish in points would be satisfactory in his first season with a brand new team. He placed fifth and was hailed as team owner of the year by many, including *The Charlotte Observer*.

Elliott took Darlington's storied Southern 500 on Labor Day weekend to snap one of the most puzzling non-winning streaks ever, at 52 races. Elliott won five times in his first season with Johnson in 1992, including the season finale. But he was shutout in all of 1993 and through the first 22 races of 1994. After problems foiled "sure looking winners" Ken Schrader and Mark Martin,

Elliott blew by Earnhardt 24 laps from the finish and pulled away to win. The victory helped Elliott wind up 10th in the final point standings.

Dale Jarrett and the Joe Gibbs Racing team took Charlotte's Mello Yello 500 in one of the biggest turnarounds on successive weekends in NASCAR history. The impressive triumph came just seven days after Jarrett had failed to qualify and missed making the field for the Holly Farms 400 at North Wilkesboro. It was the first victory in 55 races for Jarrett, who'd last won in the Daytona 500 opening the 1993 season.

Ken Schrader was the driver who made the most of a winless season, finishing fourth in the point standings as his streak without a victory stretched to 108 races dating to June of 1991. Schrader listed nine top five finishes and a solid 18 top 10s in 1994.

Morgan Shepherd and Darrell Waltrip also cracked the top 10 in the points race without winning. Shepherd finished sixth and Waltrip ninth.

While 12 drivers split the 31 victories, a record 17 drivers won poles. Geoff Bodine and Irvan tied for most no. 1 starts with five each. Ted Musgrave and rookie Loy Allen had three each. Earnhardt and Wallace paced time trials twice apiece. Winning a pole each were Martin, Rudd, Gordon, Elliott, Marlin, Mast, Spencer, rookie Ward Burton, Greg Sacks, Chuck Bown, and Harry Gant.

Gant's goal in a final season before retiring was one more Winston Cup victory. His Chevy was the strongest car in the second Pocono race, but an oil leak, which developed after Gant ran over debris, cost him that chance.

Gant wound up with no top five finishes and just seven top 10s, but bowed out as one of the most popular drivers in Winston Cup history.

Lake Speed, Michael Waltrip, Kyle Petty, Brett Bodine, Bobby Labonte, Rick Mast, Greg Sacks, and Ted Musgrave started all 31 races, but ended the season feeling they hadn't met their potential.

Todd Bodine, Jeff Burton, and Derrike Cope started 30 races each.

Jeff Burton outran older brother Ward, Joe Nemechek, John Andretti, and Steve Grissom for the rookie of the year title. He triumphed in a Ford fielded by the Stavola Brothers team on the basis of two top five finishes and three top 10s.

John Andretti made motorsports history on Memorial Day, starting both the Indianapolis 500 and the Coca-Cola 600 at Charlotte. After finishing 28th at Indy, he flew by private jet and then helicopter to the Charlotte track just in time to start the NASCAR event.

Overall, 83 drivers participated in the Winston Cup season. While deserving to be cheered for the effort, about half made little impact, failing to crack the top 10 at the finish of any race.

1. Racing Royalty for the 90's...**Dale Earnhardt** notched his seventh Winston Cup title matching King Richard's record with no end in sight.

Steve Swope

2. Waiting in the wings…**Mark Martin** won the last Winston Cup race of '94 to annex the runnerup title, one he's ready to trade in for no. 1.

Nigel Kinrade

3. Top Race Winner, Again…**Rusty Wallace** posted twice as many wins as the champion, failed to faze Earnhardt.

4. New Consistency...**Ken Schrader** collected no victories, but 18 top 10 finishes paid off handsomely in the points total.

Linda McQueeney

Nigel Kinrade

5. New Owner/Driver...**Ricky Rudd** exceeded his own forecast with a top five finish and one Winston Cup victory in his first owner/driver year.

Nigel Kinrade

6. Best Year…**Morgan Shepherd** won more than $1 million in '94 to top a 24 year career. Consistency was the key.

Dan Bianchi

7. Back in Style…**Terry Labonte**, the '84 Winston Cup champion, scored three victories, outpaced in the win column only by Wallace and Earnhardt.

8. Swift Sophomore…**Jeff Gordon**, '93 Rookie of the Year thrived on big money races, took the inaugural Brickyard 400 and the Coca-Cola 600. His $1.7 million winnings were second only to Earnhardt's.

Steve Swope

9. Regrouping for '95...**Darrell Waltrip**, a three-time Winston Cup champion, made wholesale changes in his team, targets a fourth title in '95.

10. Back to His Roots…**Bill Elliott**, for the ninth time Winston Cup's most popular driver, takes his talents (and his sponsors) back to his family team in '95 after only a single victory in '94.

Nigel Kinrade

11.

Moving Up...**Lake Speed** will be his own general manager in the Melling team in '95, after a year just outside the top 10.

12.

Best Year of the Decade...**Michael Waltrip** placed 12th in Winston Cup points, won more than $700,000 his best showing in 10 years on the circuit.

Nigel Kinrade

13.

Fast Qualifier...**Ted Musgrave**'s three '94 Virginia pole positions, two of these at Richmond, mark him as a strong contender for a first race win in '95.

Dan Bianchi

Nigel Kinrade

14.

Surprise Daytona 500 Winner...**Sterling Marlin** made his first race victory in 274 Winston Cup starts one to remember, the big one at Daytona.

Steve Swope

15.

Winless in '94...**Kyle Petty**, for the first time since 1985, failed to win a Winston Cup race in '94, a major disappointment for a driver of his established talents.

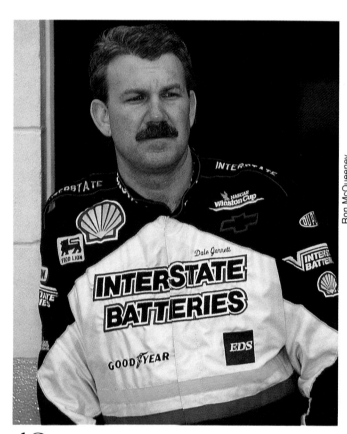

Ron McQueeney

16.

Taking Irvan's Slot...**Dale Jarrett**, the '93 Daytona 500 winner fell to engine failure in the '94 event, scored his single victory of the year in the Mello Yello 500. In '95 he moves to the Robert Yates team, replacing recovering driver Ernie Irvan.

Dan Bianchi

17.

Three Race Winner...**Geoff Bodine**, the point man for Hoosier Tires scored three Winston Cup wins, was leading the Brickyard 400 when a tangle with brother Brett took him out.

18.

Brickyard 400 Polesitter...**Rick Mast** took down the hotly contested pole position honors in the inaugural Brickyard 400, faded to 22nd at the end. He posted 10 top 10 finishes for the season.

Dan Bianchi

Dan Bianchi

19.

Replacing Bill Elliott...**Brett Bodine**, a Winston Cup race winner in 1990, managed only six top 10 finishes with the Kenny Bernstein team in '94, will move to the Junior Johnson team for '95.

20.

First Full Season...**Todd Bodine**, youngest of the three racing Bodine brothers, is looking for improved results with the Butch Mock team in '95 over 1994's seven top 10 finishes.

Ron McQueeney

ERNIE'S BACK AND TNN'S GOT HIM

Dan Bianchi

Incredible Ernie Irvan has bounced back from his life threatening Michigan practice session accident in a truly remarkable recovery. He has tested favorably in a sports car on a road circuit, admittedly not a heavier and more powerful Winston Cup stocker, on a 2.5 mile superspeedway. He debuts in February's Goodwrench 500 as a TNN commentator, a role for which he has also tested well. The Maxwell House Motorsport Spirit Award winner has been promised a ride with the Texaco-backed Robert Yates team when he's medically cleared to resume his Winston Cup driving duties.

IF THIS IS YOUR LIFE, THIS IS YOUR NETWORK.

IT DOESN'T GET ANY CLOSER.

DALE EARNHARDT'S OTHER SIDE

By Tom Higgins

Throughout his drive to a record-tying seventh NASCAR Winston Cup Series championship, Dale Earnhardt, noted for his toughness and tenacity, showed another side. He regularly evoked the memory of two men who loomed large in his life; Neil Bonnett and Ralph Earnhardt.

Bonnett, Earnhardt's best friend and hunting/fishing companion, was killed February 11, 1994 when he crashed while practicing for the Daytona 500, a race that was to begin his comeback attempt from injuries he'd suffered in 1990.

Bonnett had tested extensively for Earnhardt and the Richard Childress Racing team in 1993 and during the 1993-1994 off season. Both Earnhardt and Childress, credited Bonnett's work with being critical to their championship run in 1993.

"We're dedicating everything we do this season, and we plan to do a lot, in the memory of Neil," a saddened, shaken Earnhardt said when the awful news of Bonnett's death was confirmed that tearful afternoon at Daytona International Speedway.

Ralph Earnhardt, Dale's dad, died in 1973 of a heart attack in the same backyard shop where he'd prepared the cars he drove to two NASCAR national Sportsman Division championships.

"Everything I've achieved, all the success I've realized, I credit directly to my father," Earnhardt said in New York in December just prior to being honored for the title that tied Richard Petty's record. "I've remembered his advice through my career, and it has worked for me."

Earnhardt allowed himself a small chuckle. "I remembered except for one small thing...In the beginning, I raced on credit. I borrowed money in order to go racin'. My daddy never would have done that. He paid cash for everything he ever owned. Our house in Kannapolis (NC). His race cars and parts. His tow truck. Everything."

Dale Earnhardt lists winnings of $22,914,304 in his Winston Cup career alone, a record for all of motorsports. Because of shrewd business dealings, the eighth grade dropout probably is worth several million dollars more. Plenty of lenders would be happy to shower credit on him now, credit he doesn't need.

Earnhardt, 43, owns a Lear jet airplane, a large yacht that's based in the Bahamas, and an immaculate 300 acre ranch near Mooresville, NC, where he makes his home.

It's a cliche, but he paid his dues to earn it. While in New York, to pick up his Driver of the Year award and the huge collection of tangible and intangible honors that go with his seventh Winston Cup championship, Earnhardt smilingly recalled the early summers of his racing career, when he was learning on the dirt short tracks of the Carolinas, Georgia, and Virginia.

"I'd pull my ol' car down to Savannah, run the race, and pull it almost 300 miles back home the same night," said Earnhardt. "I'd go to my day job, I held several different ones, then come home and crawl under the race car to work on it. Lots of times I'd go to sleep tightening a bolt, then wake up with the wrench still in my hand. It was tough back then, but I wouldn't take anything for the experience. I think it played a big part in preparing me to run at the Winston Cup level."

Dale and Theresa Earnhardt

Dan Bianchi

DRIVER OF THE YEAR

Dale Earnhardt accepts the 1994 Driver of the Year award from Driver of the Year patron Ki Cuyler at New York's venerable "21" Club. Earnhardt drove his black Goodwrench Chevrolet Lumina to his seventh NASCAR Winston Cup championship, tying the previously unmatched record of "King" Richard Petty. With a new Chevrolet Monte Carlo, reportedly sporting improved aerodynamics at his disposal in '95, Earnhardt is the pre-season favorite for an eighth title.

Motorsports VIPs turned out in force to honor Earnhardt. In the foreground are International Speedway Corp.'s John Cooper, Larry Balewski, and John Graham plus Penske Racing's Dan Luginbuhl.

Dan Bianchi

Dan Bianchi

PETTY'S PICK

Richard Petty's choice for the driver's seat in his famed no. 43 STP Pontiac is Bobby Hamilton. Filling "The King's" driving shoes is challenging. Petty's seven Winston Cup titles have been matched by Dale Earnhardt, but his record six Daytona 500 victories are generally considered to be beyond reach.

TEAMS
Taming the Winston Cup Series
NASCAR'S Top Teams

Linda McQueeney

By Tom Higgins

Dale Earnhardt and his Richard Childress Racing team entered the 1994 NASCAR Winston Cup Series season heavily favored to take a second straight championship and their sixth together for four main reasons. These were: 1. Earnhardt's proven driving talent; 2. The quality and reliability of the Chevrolet equipment provided by Childress; 3. The rapport between driver and team owner, who speak warmly of "always being on the same wave length"; 4. The team's amazing stability in its roster of crew members.

Other than Kirk Shelmerdine, who resigned as crew chief after the 1992 season to pursue his own driving career, the turnover among key personnel at the Childress shop has been nil. This, in a sport where change is more the rule than the exception.

Andy Petree proved a perfect fit in moving over from the Harry Gant/Leo Jackson team to succeed Shelmerdine as team leader in 1993.

So it wasn't surprising that Earnhardt and the Childress operation contended from the season's start for a title that enabled Earnhardt to equal King Richard Petty's record seven crowns. Earnhardt essentially needed only to maintain momentum over the last 11 of the tour's 31 races to claim the title after injuries sidelined closest challenger Ernie Irvan, who trailed by a mere 27 points when he was hurt.

Longtime general mechanic and right rear tire changer Will Lind, the team comic, tired of travel at mid-season and gave up going on the road in favor of a job in the shop. His absence mainly was noted by the drop in offbeat humor around the no. 3 team's garage stalls.

Veteran engine builder Eddie Lanier, honored two of the last three seasons as NASCAR's "motor man" of the year, retired at the end of the 1994 campaign. Standing by for the promotion was assistant engine builder Danny Lawrence, elected to the season's All Pro team at that position.

Rightfully called a team without a weakness, the Earnhardt/Childress outfit continues in the favorite's role for '95.

In contrast, the situation was rather glum at Jack Roush Racing as the team finished the 1993 season. Highly regarded crew chief Steve Hmiel had taken another job, moving to Hendrick Motorsports as overseer of all three Rick Hendrick teams, fielding cars for Ken Schrader, Jeff Gordon, and newcomer Terry Labonte. Hmiel worked at the Hendrick shop only one day, turned in his notice and almost immediately resurfaced in his old job at Roush Racing.

The even-handedness of Hmiel and Martin's amazing ability to shake off deeply disappointing losses enabled the team to maintain its focus and come on for two victories in the season's second half that wrested the runnerup spot in the point standings from Rusty Wallace.

Although Wallace and the Penske South operation were edged into third place as the season wound down, many expert observers rated what the team achieved as the accomplishment of the year in Winston Cup racing.

During the 1993-94 offseason Roger Penske's NASCAR troops made a much publicized switch from Pontiacs to Fords. The changeover to Thunderbirds was undertaken although Wallace won a circuit leading 10 races in Pontiac Grand Prix automobiles in 1993.

Wallace silenced doubters by winning the second race of the season at North Carolina Motor Speedway. He then went on to triumph seven more times for eight victories overall, five more than anyone else. His performance helped give Ford the NASCAR Manufacturers' Championship for a second straight year.

As the season came to a close, crew chief Buddy Parrott was hired away to join the Diamond Ridge Racing outfit of owner Gary Bechtel and driver Steve Grissom starting in 1995. Parrott, a master motivator, had forged Wallace's pit crew into one of the fastest in the sport's history, clocking some four-tire pit stops in the 16 second range. During the offseason, Parrott's son, Brad, the Penske South tire specialist, also left the team to seek new opportunities at Hendrick Motorsports. However, chassis specialist Todd Parrott, another son, remained with the Penske team.

Although Ken Schrader didn't win a race, he finished fourth in the point standings, testimony to the efficiency of his Hendrick Motorsports team, led by South African crew chief Ken Howes. Schrader posted 18 top 10 finishes in the 31 race season.

Skeptics openly predicted that Ricky Rudd would never make it as a team owner who drove his cars. Some even went so far as to say that Rudd, starting a team from scratch, would fold the effort at some point in the season and become a "hired driver" again.

Factory brass appeared to agree, as Rudd struggled to get a deal, until Ford offered some help.

A hired driver again? Hardly. Rudd and the team he assembled along with crew chief Bill Ingle not only persevered, but performed sensationally for a brand new operation. Rudd started the '94 tour with a goal of finishing in the top 10 in the standings. He bettered that goal considerably, placing fifth and winning both a race and a pole along the way.

Rudd finished more miles than any regular running the full schedule, 12,047 of a possible 12,294, a true testimonial to reliability. The overall showing earned a $50,000 UAW-GM Teamwork Award for Ingle at season's end.

Like Schrader, veteran Morgan Shepherd and the Wood Brothers team failed to win a race, but had enough consistency and, as always, stability among personnel, to take sixth place in the point standings.

Solid leadership from Gary DeHart and Ray Everham, respectively, enabled Hendrick Motorsports drivers Terry Labonte and Jeff Gordon to win five races between them and finish seven and eight in the point standings. Labonte, new to the operation, triumphed three times to snap a four year streak without a victory. And Gordon took two of NASCAR's biggest shows, the Coca-Cola 600 at Charlotte and the inaugural Brickyard 400 at Indianapolis Motor Speedway.

Three-time Winston Cup champion, Darrell Waltrip, was another non-winner who cracked the top 10 in the point standings. He finished ninth despite a mid-season shakeup among crew members. First, the much traveled mechanic, Jake "Suitcase" Elder, left Waltrip's employ, then crew chief Barry Dodson and engine builder Lou LaRosa were let go.

Waltrip's lament of his early season woes provided one of the year's top quotes. "I'm out on a limb," he said, "and all I can hear is 35 chainsaws running."

Waltrip replaced Dodson with Clyde Booth and LaRosa with Claude Queen and wound up second to Rudd in miles completed with 12,027.

A tense relationship developed between driver Bill Elliott and team owner Junior Johnson in their third, and final, season together. However, they rode it out for a huge victory in the storied Southern 500 at historic Darlington Raceway and took 10th place in the point standings. Even before the season was over, Elliott announced that he was leaving the Johnson operation after 1994 and taking one of the team owner's key sponsors, McDonald's, with him.

Elliott returned to Dawsonville, GA, to reform his old team, led by engine-building brother Ernie. This time, the Elliotts have a fellow Georgian as a partner, Ford auto dealer Charles Hardy. The move by Elliott was one of the two biggest, among many, made by drivers for the '95 season.

In the other, Dale Jarrett won a release from Joe Gibbs Racing to take over the Robert Yates Racing ride. For now, it's a one year deal. If the injured Irvan wins a medical release to begin competition again during the season, Yates will field two Fords.

The Yates team, more than any other,

has had to deal with deep adversity the past few years. The personnel on the no. 28 team commiserated with driver Davey Allison when his father, Bobby, suffered career ending injuries in 1988. And again in '92, when Davey's brother, Clifford, was killed in a crash at Michigan International Speedway. Unbelievably, a helicopter accident took Davey himself on July 13, 1993. Then, just 13 months later, came the wreck that left Irvan with life-threatening head and lung injuries.

"I'm sure all this fits into God's plan, and it's not for us to wonder about it," said the Yates team's crew chief, Larry McReynolds. "But sometimes, it's diffi-cult not to…"

When Irvan was struck down, he'd led more times and more miles than any rival. Although he missed the last 11 races, those statistics held up for the season. Irvan led 79 times in 17 races for 2,419.5 miles.

Yates hired Kenny Wallace to fill in for the final third of the season, and Rusty's younger brother performed admirably in a difficult situation, rolling to a best showing of fourth in the Goody's 500 at Martinsville. Wallace had the Yates Thunderbird running at the finish in nine of his 10 starts.

Overall, approximately 20 teams will have different drivers in '95 as the domino theory ran amok in NASCAR.

The rundown: Lake Speed, from Bud Moore Engineering to Melling Racing as driver and general manager; Dick Trickle, from Active Racing to Moore Engineering; Mike Chase, from the Winston West Series to Active Racing; Brett Bodine, from King Racing (owned by drag racing champion Kenny Bern-stein) to Johnson's operation, succeed-ing Elliott; Steve Kinser, from sprint car racing to Bernstein; Bobby Labonte, from Bill Davis Racing to Joe Gibbs, following Jarrett; Bobby Hamilton, from SABCO

(co-owned by Felix Sabates and Dick Brooks) to Petty Enterprises; John Andretti, from Petty to the new Michael Kranefuss/Carl Haas team; Robert Pressley, from the Grand National cir-cuit to Leo Jackson Motorsports, suc-ceeding the retired Harry Gant.

Also: Joe Nemechek, from Larry Hedrick Motorsports to his own team; Ricky Craven, from Grand National to Hedrick; Jimmy Spencer, from Johnson to Smokin' Joe Racing (Travis Carter); Loy Allen, from Tri-Star Motorsports to Johnson, succeeding Spencer; Greg Sacks, from U.S. Racing/D.K. Ulrich to SABCO, taking Hamilton's former ride; Davy Jones, from IndyCar and

IMSA to Ulrich; Bobby Hillin, from free-lancing to Moroso Racing; Randy LaJoie, from Moroso to Bill Davis, following Bobby Labonte.

Additionally, Kenny Wallace, the Grand National tour's most popular driver, and his Filmar Racing team will move en masse to the Winston Cup tour.

Unlike Elliott and the others, Wally Dallenbach, Jr., didn't wait until sea-son's end to be involved in a change. Dallenbach left Richard Petty's employ as driver following the road course race at Watkins Glen, NY, in August and was replaced by Andretti. Andretti became available when team owner Billy Hagan ceased operations to reorganize and seek a sponsor.

In another in-season change, Sabates released veteran Robin Pemberton as team manager for driver Kyle Petty. Dodson, who had been off Waltrip's payroll for only a matter of days, was hired to replace Pemberton.

As expected, Pemberton shortly was hired by Jack Roush to serve as crew chief for the team servicing Ted Mus-grave. Pemberton spent the 1988-91 seasons with Roush, co-leading the teams of Mark Martin and Hmiel.

Only days after the '94 season ended, Penske and Wallace hired Pemberton to change teams again and succeed the colorful Parrott.

Similarly, the Stavola Brothers team that fields Fords for 1994 rookie of the year Jeff Burton hired Donnie Richeson to become crew chief. Richeson left the same position at King Racing, and ten-tative plans were for team manager Richard Broome to fill both roles.

Nigel Kinrade

Fast Exit. Rusty Wallace hustles past the still-stopped trio of Jeff Gordon, Bill Elliott, and Sterling Marlin.

Wish Denied. What Harry Gant wanted most in his final NASCAR season in a career spanning three decades was one more Winston Cup victory, his 19th. His best efforts and those of his Leo Jackson team fell short. A pole at Bristol proved that the popular driver was leaving the circuit with skills intact.

Full House. Packed pit lane at the Goodwrench 500 places heavy emphasis on rapid refueling and tire changes.

Nigel Kinrade

36th DAYTONA 500

Sterling Marlin's first Winston Cup win is the big one.

Winston Cup Race 1
Daytona Beach, FL
February 20, 1994

By Tom Higgins

After 18 years and 278 previous NASCAR Winston Cup races without a checkered flag, Sterling Marlin glittered and scored one of the most popular Daytona 500 victories in history.

Although low fuel was a concern among all the frontrunners, Marlin nevertheless held his Chevrolet wide open during the dramatic closing laps at Daytona International Speedway and fended off Ford foe Ernie Irvan for his first triumph.

The drawling winner from Columbia, TN., son of colorful former NASCAR driver Coo Coo Marlin, finished stock car racing's biggest show a scant 19-hundredths of a second in front, or about two car lengths.

Ironically, Marlin now drives for the Morgan/McClure Motorsports team that Irvan left amid some controversy in September of 1993 in order to join Robert Yates Racing.

The driving duo also finished 1-2 in the 500 of 1991 with Irvan winning for the Morgan/McClure team.

Marlin's first victory came in his initial start for the Larry McClure-led operation based in Abingdon, VA.

Team co-owner Tim Morgan had figured the fuel mileage perfectly. He calculated that Marlin, after pitting for the final time on lap 141, had just enough gasoline to go the final 59 laps, or 147.5 miles.

Marlin, who led 30 laps, went in front for keeps on lap 180 when Irvan's car bobbled slightly coming off turn 4 at the famous 2.5-mile track.

"Tony told me by radio we had enough fuel to make it the distance and I never second-guessed it," said Marlin. "I held it wide open and didn't worry about saving gas. I didn't have to lift off the throttle after we got the car to handling right about midway of the race and that was the key. If I'd have had to lift, Ernie would have got by me."

Asked to describe his thoughts during the last lap—when Irvan closed fast in the Ford in which he led 84 laps—Marlin joked, "Well, it seemed like it was a *long* lap.

"I just told myself it was a short track Saturday night at Nashville and there ain't nothing to it."

Marlin, 36, is a former Nashville

Raceway track champion.

He became the ninth different Daytona 500 winner in as many years and the fourth in the event's 36-year history to get his first victory at NASCAR's top level in the classic, joining Derrike Cope (1990), Pete Hamilton ('70), Mario Andretti ('67) and the late Tiny Lund ('63) in that category.

Marlin averaged 156.931 mph in earning $253,275. His victory put the Morgan/McClure team on the NASCAR Winners' Circle plan, worth $300,000 in appearance money over the rest of the 31-race season in 1994.

Terry Labonte making his first start in the Hendrick Motorsports team's Chevy, took third place about 10 car lengths back of Irvan. Labonte's teammate, Jeff Gordon, finished fourth and Ford veteran Morgan Shepherd was fifth.

Completing the top 10: Greg Sacks, Ford; Dale Earnhardt, Chevy; Ricky Rudd, Ford; Bill Elliott, Ford; and Ken Schrader, Chevy.

Nigel Kinrade

GOODWRENCH 500
Winston Cup Race 2
Rockingham, NC
February 27, 1994

Rusty Wallace, new Ford take the Goodwrench 500 in style.

Any doubts that Rusty Wallace, who notched his ten '93 victories in Pontiacs, could win at the wheel of Fords in '94 evaporated in the sunshine of the winner's circle in the Goodwrench 500. Wallace even predicted that Ford would win the '94 manufacturer's title, a prediction that held up at season end. His prediction on the '94 Winston Cup champion did not fare so well. Wallace clearly had the race in hand, a practice that is becoming habitual, since he won both '93 Winston Cup races at Rockingham. His margin of superiority was evident in that he led 70% of the 492 laps.

Daytona 500 winner Sterling Marlin had another good outing, finishing second by just over five seconds and holding his early season lead in the Winston Cup points chase. Rick Mast, Mark Martin, and Ernie Irvan rounded out the top five, the latter two a lap down.

PONTIAC 400
Winston Cup Race 3
Richmond, VA
March 6, 1994

Ernie Irvan beats Rusty Wallace in a battle of pit stops.

Ernie Irvan's Texaco-backed team faced down Rusty Wallace's crew in two late race pit stop duels that put Irvan in the Pontiac 400 winner's circle. The first head-to-head confrontation in the pits put Irvan out front, the second kept him there. Both the leading Ford drivers enjoyed excellent handling and bountiful horsepower. Jeff Gordon, the third place finisher, might have been a contender at the end except for a pit crew miscue that sent him out with a loose wheel. Fourth place Dale Earnhardt had no complaints, felt he got what his car was capable of, as did fifth place Kyle Petty. Mark Martin, Rick Mast, Brett Bodine, and Terry LaBonte, occupying sixth through ninth places at the finish, all completed the scheduled 400 laps.

Nigel Kinrade

PUROLATOR 500
Winston Cup Race 4
Atlanta, GA
March 13, 1994

Two in a row for Irvan.

Colorful Californian Ernie Irvan had the makings of a mini-roll going for him in the Purolator 500. Even an overly quick departure from the pits on lap 155, with two lug nuts loose couldn't keep him out of victory circle for two in a row in '94 and his 11th win since he joined the Winston Cup tour. Corrective action taken, Irvan led for all but two of the last 99 laps. Morgan Shepherd posted a well-earned second place. Of technical interest, third place Darrell Waltrip and fourth place Jeff Burton, a rookie, were on Hoosier tires, con-

testing a long reign of Goodyear dominance. So were the top two qualifiers, Loy Allen and Geoff Bodine. Only the first four finishers completed all 328 laps. '93 Winston Cup champion Dale Earnhardt continued his slow season start, didn't make the top 10. Nobody is counting him out, with 27 races yet to run.

TRANSOUTH 400
Winston Cup Race 5
Darlington, SC
March 27, 1994

Earnhardt tops the Darlington field, again.

It was only a matter of time until Dale Earnhardt won another race. For the '93 Winston Cup champion

that time had dragged on too long, 16 races, since the previous July. Earnhardt enthusiasts were quick to note that four of his five TranSouth wins led to Winston Cup titles. The track that drivers consider the toughest on the circuit has now been tamed nine times by Earnhardt. Mark Martin in the Valvoline Ford placed second, down 7.4 seconds to Earnhardt's Chevrolet. Ernie Irvan, the points leader, was in second place when a penalty for having too many crew members over the wall cost him any chance at victory. Rusty Wallace was slowed by a pit stop miscue and was forced out of contention by a cut tire which caused a crash. Polesitter Bill Elliott placed third, his best showing of the year, while Dale Jarrett and Lake Speed rounded out the top five.

FOOD CITY 500
Winston Cup Race 6
Bristol, TN
April 10, 1994

Earnhardt survives crash-laden
Food City 500.

Dale Earnhardt had no illusions
about how he arrived in the winner's
circle at Bristol: "We didn't have 'em
covered, just caught the cautions
right." The caution he caught most
fortuitously was the yellow at lap 318.
Second and third place finishers Ken
Schrader and Lake Speed caught
it, too. Less fortunate were Geoff
Bodine, the leader at lap 300, Mark
Martin, Bobby Labonte, and Jeff
Gordon who didn't. Bodine ended up
a lap down in fourth place, the others
were even further in arrears. No less
than nine cars were knocked out by
accidents, including Ricky Rudd,
Gordon, Martin, Harry Gant, Dale
Jarrett, Jeff Burton, Bill Elliott, and
Rick Mast. 18 cars were circulating
with visible battle damage at the
end, among them record setting
polesitter Chuck Bown's Ford. With
Earnhardt's second win in a row went
the Winston Cup points lead, demoting Ernie Irvan to second place.

FIRST UNION 400
Winston Cup Race 7
North Wilkesboro, NC
April 17, 1994

Terry Labonte's win,
his first in five years.

The Winston Cup champion in
1984, Terry Labonte had fallen on
lean times without a single victory
over the past five years and 134 previous starts. His trip to victory circle
might have taken even longer except
for a pit stop miscalculation by Ernie
Irvan who "owned" the race for the
first 328 laps of the 400 scheduled.
The dashing Texaco-backed driver
set a new record to claim the pole
and was out in front for 320 laps. In
the pits for a routine yellow flag stop,
Irvan failed to wait long enough while
the left rear tire was being changed.
The ensuing confusion dropped him
from first to fifth and the best he
could do at the end was third. Winner
Labonte was candid, "Except for the
yellow flag Ernie could have lapped
the field." The miscue allowed Winston Cup points leader Earnhardt,
who finished fifth, to retain a 20
point lead over Irvan. Rusty Wallace
took down second place, Kyle Petty
placed fourth.

Nigel Kinrade

Nigel Kinrade

HANES 500
Winston Cup Race 8
Martinsville, VA
April 24, 1994

Rusty Wallace beats a speeding ticket, wins Hanes 500.

Rusty Wallace's "speeding ticket" wasn't handed to him on the way to the track, didn't involve a fine, but could have been the most expensive citation he ever received. Nabbed by NASCAR's traffic cops for exceeding the speed limit on the Martinsville Speedway pit lane, he was shunted from first place, after leading 255 of the first 322 laps, to eighth place. More importantly he was now 25th in a long line of cars on the tight, difficult-to-pass, half-mile track. Not lost on the distraught driver of the Miller-backed Ford was the almost certain loss of the nearly $100,000 bonus he could claim from Unocal for winning from the pole position. Not to worry, team owner Roger Penske, possessed of a racing mind

second to none was on hand to talk Wallace out of his dilemma, which is exactly what he did, with a little help from Geoff Bodine who crashed on lap 387. Fast yellow flag pit work elevated Wallace to fourth place. Wallace then passed Darrell Waltrip and Mark Martin to gain second place. The final caution on lap 433 saw the Penske crew again on top, beating leader Ernie Irvan out of the pits. Irvan gained the Winston Cup points lead for his efforts. Martin, Waltrip, and Morgan Shepherd filled in the other top five positions.

WINSTON SELECT 500
Winston Cup Race 9
Talladega, AL
May 1, 1994

Dale Earnhardt nips Ernie Irvan in the "best Talladega race ever".

Even Dale Earnhardt called it, "the most exciting Talladega race I've ever

been in," and he has won six times previously at the big, fast Alabama circuit. With only 25 laps of the scheduled 188 remaining, Earnhardt's chances of winning from 11th place looked dim indeed. With five laps left, an all out charge, capped by his pass of Jimmy Spencer, a driver not noted for being "easy" to get by, was the key element in the victory. Now, all he had to contend with were Ernie Irvan, Michael Waltrip, and Ken Schrader, on his tail in earnest in addition to a disgruntled Spencer. Somehow he held off this voracious quartet, beating Irvan the polesitter and Waltrip by the slimmest margin. The finish line camera was required to separate Spencer and Schrader into fourth and fifth places. Spencer admitted some culpability in the early accident that eliminated Terry Labonte, Dick Trickle, Jeff Purvis, Wally Dallenbach, Jr., Rusty Wallace, Derrike Cope, and Jimmy Hensley but dismissed charges that he was "too aggressive". Surprisingly, the first 18 drivers to finish were on the lead lap.

TALLADEGA AL

Nigel Kinrade

SAVE MART 300
Winston Cup Race 10
Sonoma, CA
May 15, 1994

Ernie Irvan masters Sears Point
road course, repeats
'92 victory.

Ernie Irvan is unlikely to be held up as a role model for budding Formula One drivers, but when it comes to muscling a stock car around a road course, he has few peers. But then he doesn't have too many on the big oval tracks either, Irvan is simply a certified racer. His second Sears Point win in three years was from the pole. The native Californian was in command all day. Not even Ricky Rudd and Rusty Wallace, NASCAR's acknowledged top road course talents could mount a serious challenge. The stiffest opposition came from second place Geoff Bodine, whose Hoosier tires seemed to offer some advantage in the middle of the pit stop cycle. Dale Earnhardt had one of his best ever road course outings, finishing a solid third, followed by STP-backed Wally Dallenbach, Jr., in his best effort of '94, and Rusty Wallace. Clearly the day was Irvan's as it enhanced his Winston Cup points lead over Earnhardt to 40 markers.

COCA-COLA 600
Winston Cup Race 11
Charlotte, NC '
May 29, 1994

Gordon's gamble gains the
victory in rich Coca-Cola 600.

"Golden boy" Jeff Gordon parlayed third position and a high risk late race gamble on a two tire pit stop into his first points paying Winston Cup victory. As luck would have it, this all took place in the $1.3 million Coca-Cola 600 instead of a shorter event with a fraction of the prize money. On lap 380, race leader Rusty Wallace and second place Geoff Bodine pitted taking on four tires and fuel. Meanwhile, Gordon's crew chief Ray Everham cooly called for two tires and fuel. The under nine second stop got Gordon out ahead of Wallace and Bodine. Gordon took the top spot when new leader Ricky Rudd had to pit for a splash of fuel. To Gordon's credit, he held off some top opposition in the final 10 laps to claim the victory. Wallace, Bodine, Dale Jarrett, and Ernie Irvan finished in his wake. Wallace's camp was disconsolate at being outmaneuvered. Rusty's crew chief Buddy Parrott admitted, "We should have changed two and won by a ton."

BUDWEISER 500
Winston Cup Race 12
Dover, DE
June 5, 1994

Rusty Wallace tames a slick
Dover track for third '94 win.

Rusty Wallace, abetted by his talented Penske South crew mastered a slick Dover Downs racing surface for his third win of '94, matching points leaders Ernie Irvan and Dale Earnhardt in the victory column. A platoon of other drivers weren't as lucky. The accident list included Harry Gant, Geoff Bodine, Jimmy Spencer, Dick Trickle, Ward Burton, Billy Standridge, Ted Musgrave, Bobby Hamilton, Jeff Burton, Brett Bodine, Dale Jarrett, Dale Earnhardt, Steve Grissom, Morgan Shepherd, Greg Sacks, Derrike Cope, John Andretti, Chuck Bown, Bobby Labonte, and Dave Marcis. In short, half the field was sidelined or impeded. Mark Martin, who finished fourth just behind Ken Schrader and ahead of Jeff Gordon, called the surface "unfit for racing". Second place Irvan admitted that he "rode out the last 100 laps" rather than risking a serious move on Wallace. His caution paid off. He's now 163 points ahead of Earnhardt in the Winston Cup chase.

Nigel Kinrade

UAW-GM TEAMWORK 500
Winston Cup Race 13
Long Pond, PA
June 12, 1994

Rusty Wallace salvages
Pocono win.

Race dominating Rusty Wallace had to be wondering how a 23 second lead with seven laps to go turned into a dicey second place with six laps to go and the race under caution. How it happened was a yellow flag when Mark Martin blew a tire on lap 194. Then second place Dale Earnhardt took on only two tires and got out ahead of Wallace whose crew opted for four. With six laps left, the better shod Wallace should have been able to get by handily, except that third place Jeff Gordon spun under caution and insisted on regaining his third place under yellow to the consternation of the NASCAR officials. With only one lap to go the officials flashed the green plus white flags…"Go racing, one lap left." Wallace got by Earnhardt with a margin of .28 seconds. Gordon, third on the track, was officially demoted to sixth place. Ken Schrader, Morgan Shepherd, and Mark Martin filled in the top five places.

MILLER 400
Winston Cup Race 14
Brooklyn, MI
June 19, 1994

Rusty Wallace makes it
three in a row at Michigan.

On a three race roll that made him June's dominant driver, Rusty Wallace overcame late race fuel problems to capture the Miller Genuine Draft 400. It should have been easier. However, Wallace's car ran out of fuel, when a caution flag on lap 175 forced him to take an extra lap. To add to this problem, his engine balked and refused to refire, finally responding to crew chief Buddy Parrott's ministrations. When he did get out, Wallace was in 12th place, but with four laps to go, got up to second and handily passed Earnhardt for the lead. For the second race in a row, he had vanquished the toughest competitor in the trade at the very end.

Mark Martin, Ricky Rudd, and Morgan Shepherd completed the top five. Based on his '94 record, the racing gods like to test Wallace by denying him, at the last minute, the routine win he would seem to have earned earlier in the contest.

PEPSI 400
Winston Cup Race 15
Daytona Beach, FL
July 2, 1994

Jimmy Spencer notches
first win in Pepsi 400

After enduring 128 winless starts and competitor complaints about his driving tactics too numerous to tally, Jimmy Spencer won the Pepsi 400 in storybook style. He passed point man Ernie Irvan in turn two of the last lap, battled the Winston Cup points leader fender-to-fender through the last two turns to reach the finish line in front by less than half a car length. In addition to the victory, he garnered the cheers of the close knit Winston Cup fraternity. These accolades may have meant as much to Spencer as his first Winston Cup winner's purse. Dale Earnhardt, Mark Martin, and Ken Schrader rounded out the top five. Jimmy Spencer has always earned his "Mr. Excitement" title. Today he earned some respect to go with it.

The race's one major crash, on lap 119, involved Joe Nemecek, Brett Bodine, Jeremy Mayfield, Ted Musgrave, Bobby Hamilton, and Jimmy Hensley.

SLICK-50 300K
Winston Cup Race 16
Loudon, NH
July 10, 1994

Ricky Rudd avoids the marbles, wins New Hampshire's Slick-50.

Aptly named, the Slick-50 300K was contested on an ultra-slippery New Hampshire International Speedway and new owner/driver Ricky Rudd mastered the marbles better than any other driver. That included '93 Winston Cup champion Dale Earnhardt, who was demoted to second place by a smooth Rudd pass with five laps to go—and polesitter Ernie Irvan, who led 174 laps while dominating the first half of the race but fell victim to the "marbles" on lap 277. The victory kept intact Rudd's streak of at least one win in each of his twelve years on the circuit. Among active drivers, only Earnhardt has a longer streak going. Rudd, who qualified third, and stayed near the top all day generously and correctly accorded crew chief Billy Ingle with the call that notched the win, Ingle's first ever. A two-tire change pit stop on lap 266 when other leaders took on four made the difference. Rusty Wallace, Mark Martin, and Todd Bodine were the other top five finishers.

MILLER 500
Winston Cup Race 17
Long Pond, PA
July 17, 1994

Geoff Bodine leads a Hoosier sweep at Pocono.

Hoosier Tire protagonist Geoff Bodine found his loyalty rewarded in the Miller Genuine Draft 500 at Pocono. He led a Hoosier shod quartet across the line from the pole. Three rookies were next in line after the flying Bodine, Ward Burton, Joe Nemechek, and Jeff Burton. Top Goodyear user was fifth place Morgan Shepherd. Sentimental favorite Harry Gant, in his last season on the circuit, led twice, spun out of contention, victimized by a faulty oil line fitting. Seventh place Dale Earnhardt added to his points lead when top contender Ernie Irvan failed to finish for the second race in a row. Rusty Wallace still lurks in third place in the Winston Cup standings, followed by Mark Martin and Morgan Shepherd. Bodine was doubly happy since it was his first win since taking over the former Alan Kulwicki team as owner/driver.

Nigel Kinrade

DIEHARD 500
Winston Cup Race 18
Talladega, AL
July 24, 1994

Jimmy Spencer loves superspeedways, takes Talladega's DieHard 500.

Scoring the first one-two for the Junior Johnson team in a decade, "Mr. Excitement" Jimmy Spencer led teammate Bill Elliott across the Talladega finish line by a mere 0.025 seconds. Despite the close finish, fans anticipating a fender-to-fender countdown between pole-sitter Dale Earnhardt and ardent rival Spencer were disappointed. Earnhardt bowed out with a burned piston after 80 laps. Geoff Bodine, Joe Nemechek, Rusty Wallace, and Dale Jarrett joined Earnhardt on the sidelines with a variety of mechanical ailments. Ernie Irvan who led the most laps, 90, finished third, regaining the Winston Cup point lead from Earnhardt. Spencer, displaying new polish, frustrated every move that Elliott made on him in the last 19 laps, after taking the lead on lap 170. Ken Schrader notched fourth place and Sterling Marlin completed the top five. Spencer's victory placed him in the elite company of Earnhardt, Wallace, and Irvan, the only other drivers to win two or more '94 races.

Ron McQueeney

Paul Webb

BRICKYARD 400
Winston Cup Race 19
Indianapolis, IN
August 6, 1994

Hometown hero Jeff Gordon
wins the inaugural
Brickyard 400, $613,000.

Fast—and fortunate—Jeff Gordon
won the most anticipated single race
in NASCAR history, the first ever
Winston Cup event at the hallowed
Indianapolis Motor Speedway before
an estimated 300,000 fans. Fast; he
led 93 of the 160 laps scheduled.
Fortunate; Ernie Irvan who led 20 of
the last 25 laps, cut a tire at this point,
went a lap down. Geoff Bodine, who
could have been a factor at the end
was punted into the wall by brother
Brett while in the lead. Brett survived
the tangle to finish second. Dale
Earnhardt, disappointed at qualifying
second, instead of on the pole,
scraped the wall on the first lap, could
recover only to fifth place. Polesitter
Rick Mast encountered electrical problems, wound up 22nd, a lap down.

None of these misfortunes detracts
from the flawless performance of the
DuPont-backed Chevrolet driver, who
just turned 23 two days before the
race. Chevrolet General Manager
and GM Vice President Jim Perkins
helped Gordon celebrate both events
in the victory circle.

IMS photo/Dan Boyd

Hometown hero, Jeff Gordon, is flanked in the inaugural Brickyard 400 winner's circle by his fiancee, Brooke Sealy, and Jim Perkins, GM Vice President and General Manager of the Chevrolet Division. The raised arm in the background belongs to Herb Fishel, head of GM's Motorsports Technology Group responsible for the racing development of Gordon's Lumina and the others on the circuit.

Steve Swope

Nigel Kinrade

BUD AT THE GLEN
Winston Cup Race 20
Watkins Glen, NY
August 14, 1994
Mark Martin wins
from the pole, again.

Easily matching his '93 victory here, Mark Martin took down pole position and top honors in the Bud at the Glen. The win was easier than the 0.88 second edge his Valvoline backed, Jack Roush prepared Ford clocked over second place Ernie Irvan, who started fourth. Though Martin's smooth, rhythmic style contrasts with Irvan's curb-bashing approach, the pair have excellent road racing records. Dale Earnhardt, who prefers oval tracks, but applies himself assiduously to road circuits as well, had a good day, starting sixth, finishing third, and ably defending his lead over Irvan in the Winston Cup points chase. Ken Schrader, who started second, ended up fourth, with Ricky Rudd, an ac-

complished road racer taking down the last top five slot. Irvan admitted that the yellow flag with nine laps to go allowed him to get close, but that Martin had a clear edge when the green came out. Wally Dallenbach, in his last drive for the STP backed Richard Petty team, was in fourth place on lap 85, went off the track trying to get by third place Rusty Wallace, later collided with him taking both drivers out of contention.

GM GOODWRENCH
DEALERS 400
Winston Cup Race 21
Brooklyn, MI
August 21, 1994
Geoff Bodine's Michigan win
overshadowed by Irvan's crash.

Ernie Irvan, battling Dale Earnhardt for the Winston Cup points lead all year, faced a different and more chilling fight this weekend. First, for his life, after a startling practice session crash into Michigan Inter-

national Speedway's turn two wall when he was coming in to correct a "push". Second, for a return of the physical and personal talent that made him one of NASCAR's best and most charismatic drivers. Preliminary medical opinion was that Irvan would win his first test, but opinions on his return as a top line driver were guarded. The race started on a somber note, not eased by a major first lap crash, initiated by Derrike Cope and Billy Standridge, and involving six "innocents", Dale Jarrett, Bobby Hillin Jr., Jeff Burton, Dick Trickle, Phil Parsons, and Morgan Shepherd. Jarrett called the first lap tangle "stupid". When the green flag waved again, Geoff Bodine went to the front and stayed in command. "He was playing with us," commented second place finisher Mark Martin. Rick Mast, Rusty Wallace, and Bobby Labonte completed the top five. Richard Petty's new driver, John Andretti, qualified well but failed to finish in the top ten.

Double Duty. Penske team's meticulously prepared, Mobil-lubed Chevy propelled Rusty Wallace to eight Winston Cup victories. Too often the raceday crew had the unhappy task of patching up accident damage not of their driver's making.

Nigel Kinrade

Nigel Kinrade

GOODY'S 300
Winston Cup Race 22
Bristol, TN
August 27, 1994

Rusty Wallace notches nighttime win at Bristol.

Working his day job, Rusty Wallace has posted three victories on Bristol's short track, with its heavy emphasis on handling. Working his night job, he added another win under the lights. Wallace got a big assist from Geoff Bodine who dropped out after leading 168 laps and seemingly on his way to his second win in a row. Wallace got a second assist from brother Mike, who held up second finisher Mark Martin with ten laps to go—if you accept Martin's version of the incident. The Wallace sibling pleaded innocent of any unsporting conduct. "I got my butt chewed out by Mark after the race, but in no way did I intend anything to happen to him."

Dale Earnhardt scored more useful Winston Cup points with a third place finish. With second place title contender Ernie Irvan certainly out for the remainder of the season, his closest pursuers become Martin and Rusty Wallace, both more than 200 markers in arrears. Darrell Waltrip and Bill Elliott rounded out the top five. A third Wallace brother, Kenny, replacing seriously injured Irvan in his Texaco-backed ride, finished 13th.

MOUNTAIN DEW 500
Winston Cup Race 23
Darlington, SC
September 4, 1994

Bill Elliott is back in victory circle at Darlington.

Shut out of victory circle for the entire '93 season, and two-thirds of the '94 calendar, Bill Elliott's return to the win column on NASCAR's "toughest track" was highly welcome to the perennial "Most Popular Driver". The win was also highly unusual, in that he passed Dale Earnhardt with 13 laps to go, powered by an engine that was overheating and threatening to blow up for the last 100 laps. Perhaps Earnhardt's engine was threatening him even more sternly. The highly abrasive track chewed little chunks of rubber out of the tires, making for clogged radiators and inevitable overheating. An even dozen of competitors dropped out of the contest with overheating or related engine problems. The principal victims were Ken Schrader who led 127 laps and Mark Martin who posted 105 laps in front. Geoff Bodine, on the pole for the fourth time this year, was among the victims, completing only 323 of the 367 laps scheduled. Morgan Shepherd, Ricky Rudd, and Sterling Marlin kept their cool, rounded out the top five.

MILLER 400
Winston Cup Race 24
Richmond, VA
September 10, 1994

Terry Labonte shrugs off rain delay, wins the Miller 400.

NASCAR has no 24 hour endurance races, but they do sanction nighttime events, under the lights to be sure, and at Richmond they had one that carried over into a second day—by a matter of minutes. Totally unfazed by the hour and a half rain delay and the 9 p.m. starting time, Terry Labonte relentlessly and, seemingly effortlessly, ran down leader Rusty Wallace for good with 27 laps to go. Labonte's Hendricks Racing teammate Jeff Gordon then vaulted over a slightly fading Wallace for second place. Wallace ended up fourth. His eye on a seventh Winston Cup, only seven races away, Dale Earnhardt was consistency itself, took a solid third place. He now leads Wallace by 232 points and Mark Martin by 303. Ricky Rudd, fifth today and having a highly successful first season as owner/driver, occupies fourth place, down 410 points, has literally no chance. Earnhardt is too much of a realist to make any premature statement on his title odds, but his supporters have already written his name on Winston Cup '94.

SPLITFIRE 500
Winston Cup Race 25
Dover, DE
September 18, 1994

Rusty Wallace wins
Splitfire 500 under yellow.

NASCAR officials (and most fans) don't like yellow flag finishes, but, despite their best efforts, they got one in Dover's Splitfire 500. The winner, engine sputtering on a low fuel supply, limping home in front on a flat tire was Rusty Wallace. None of his previous six wins this season was as bizarre. Trailing leader Mark Martin by a hefty seven seconds with 30 laps to go Wallace's chances appeared slim. At the 21 laps to go juncture, Martin tapped Ricky Rudd while lapping him. Martin stayed in front until blowing a tire and crashing with just six laps left. Martin's misfortune vaulted Wallace into the

lead. With four laps to go his engine started to sputter, so he went down to the apron hoping to pick up more fuel. He *did* pick up more fuel but with it an unwanted flat tire due to debris. With two laps to go, NASCAR officials tried their best to signal a restart, had to call the effort off when Rick Mast and Sterling Marlin ran out of fuel. Wallace called his win, "A miracle." He was right. In the top five; Earnhardt, Darrell Waltrip, Ken Schrader, and Geoff Bodine.

GOODY'S 500
Winston Cup Race 26
Martinsville, VA
September 25, 1994

Two in a row, Rusty Wallace
dominates the Goody's 500.

No miracle needed this time. Rusty Wallace just plain outdrove the entire Goody's 500 field at Martinsville. That

includes almost certain champion-to-be Dale Earnhardt who registered a snug second place, despite spinning out twice. His latest two wins, for a season high total of eight, netted Wallace only 10 Winston Cup points in his struggle against Earnhardt for the Winston Cup title. Bill Elliott took down third place. Kenny Wallace and Dale Jarrett rounded out the top five. Neither of Earnhardt's spins from which he recovered admirably were of his own making. Kenny Wallace and Rick Mast were the instigators. Wallace and Earnhardt put on a crowd pleasing short track battle to the end over the last 28 laps, the nod going to Wallace. Earnhardt noted, "I was doing all I could, but I needed a few more laps." Wallace admitted to being thoroughly concerned about Earnhardt. "I couldn't shake him til the very end."

TYSON HOLLY FARMS 400
Winston Cup Race 27
North Wilkesboro, NC
October 2, 1994

Geoff Bodine laps the field.

"Never had a day like this day. Never touched the car, it was that good," proclaimed a jubilant Geoff Bodine in the Tyson Holly Farms 400 winner's circle at North Wilkesboro. It might be a while before he (or any of his competitors) has another day this good since the last time the winner lapped the entire field was back in 1991. Only once was Bodine's win in jeopardy. On lap 351, on a restart, Rusty Wallace, trying to get back on the same lap as the leader, tagged Bodine in the fourth turn. Bodine got straightened out from a sideways posture and never again was threatened. Bodine's 335 laps in the lead, occurred in two stages, laps 48 through 81 and 100 through the last of the 400 scheduled.

Jimmy Spencer added another milestone to his best ever year by taking the pole. After five laps in front he faded, far out of contention. Terry Labonte, Rick Mast, and Rusty Wallace, finishing second through fourth were a lap down. Fifth place Mark Martin was an additional lap short of the flying Bodine. The clear cut victory took some, but not all, of the sting out of Bodine's 12 DNFs for the season to date.

MELLO YELLO 500
Winston Cup Race 28
Concord, NC
October 9, 1994

Dale Jarrett's first win of '94 comes at Concord.

Not even a finish under caution could take the edge off Dale Jarrett's first Winston Cup victory since the Daytona 500 of '93. Jarrett's big break in the Mello Yello 500 came when Ricky Rudd and Jeff Gordon tangled on lap 325. On the green flag lap, 331, Jarrett managed to pass leader Morgan Shepherd and held him off until another yellow, with two laps left of the 334 scheduled, handed Jarrett the victory. This final caution was triggered by an intra-family collision. The Waltrips, Michael and Darrell, played the lead roles in this unwanted family get together. The race started out as another Bodine run away with 202 laps of the first 290 in the lead. Brett Bodine then took over for 10 laps before handing the lead to Ken Schrader who turned it over to Morgan Shepherd.

NASCAR officials later deemed Rudd to be the aggressor in his encounter with Gordon, fined him $10,000 and put him on suspension for the balance of the season. Dale Earnhardt's solid third place put him in striking distance of the '94 Winston Cup, perhaps as soon as the AC-Delco 500 at Rockingham in two weeks.

Nigel Kinrade

AC-DELCO 500
Winston Cup Race 29
Rockingham, NC
October 23, 1994

Dale Earnhardt wins his seventh Winston Cup—early and in style.

It's all over for '94. Dale Earnhardt notched his seventh Winston Cup championship in the AC-Delco 500 at Rockingham, with two races left on the calendar. Not for Earnhardt to back into the title as he could have, based on his nearly insurmountable point lead. Instead, he put his Goodwrench Chevrolet in front for 108 laps, 77 of these at the end, to win by two car lengths. It wasn't the first time Earnhardt took the title early. In 1986, he won with one race left to go, in 1987, with two races still scheduled. Earnhardt's winning margin over Rick Mast was only a couple of car lengths, with third place Morgan Shepherd, polesitter Ricky Rudd, Terry Labonte, and Bill Elliott clustered close astern. An unhappy Rusty Wallace lost his engine on lap 300, now will have to struggle to maintain his second place in the Winston Cup points standings. Magnanimous in victory as he is taciturn in defeat, Earnhardt acknowledged the only previous seven time champion Richard Petty as "The King". "Richard got us here. He'll *always* be The King. It's unbelievable what he's done for racing." The repaved track was *fast*. Every qualifier broke the old lap record.

SLICK-50 500K
Winston Cup Race 30
Phoenix, AZ
October 30, 1994

Terry Labonte posts his third '94 victory in the Slick-50 500K.

The Winston Cup title is already wrapped up, but Terry Labonte set his sights on his third win of the year and scored handily at Phoenix. Labonte credited his last set of Goodyears with the victory after a lead-swapping battle with second place finisher Mark Martin. Martin concurred. "My last set of tires was loose. We couldn't catch Labonte." Sterling Marlin, the polesitter, was third. The race was marked by two unusual incidents. It was stopped for 26 minutes to repair a three foot hole in the wall put there by John Andretti early in the race. The second involved Jimmy Spencer who on exiting his car after a spin was confronted by car owner D.K. Ulrich who blamed Mr. Excitement for spinning out his driver earlier in the race. NASCAR officials separated the pair. New champion Dale Earnhardt lasted only 91 laps, consoled by the fact that his title was already in the bag. Rusty Wallace finished 17th, slipping in his bid to retain second place in the Winston Cup points chase. Jeff Gordon and Ted Musgrave rounded out the top five.

HOOTERS 500
Winston Cup Race 31
Atlanta, GA
November 13, 1994

Mark Martin's season ending victory augurs well for '95.

A perennial candidate for Winston Cup title honors, Mark Martin gained some solace for his failed '94 attempt in winning the Hooters 500 at Atlanta. His victory, coupled with Rusty Wallace's 32nd place finish, enabled him to vault into second place in the season's standings, worth $115,000 more than the $235,000 that goes to the third place driver in the Winston Cup championship. The $104,200 first place prize money for the Hooters 500 win was a source of additional cheer. Perhaps, most importantly, Martin and his Valvoline backed, Ford mounted Jack Roush team ended the season on a high note, well poised for the opening '95 round, the Daytona 500 a mere three months away. Lest Martin get too confident, new champion Dale Earnhardt sent a reminder that he's not going away soon by finishing a solid second, after starting 30th. Three Ford drivers, Todd Bodine, Lake Speed, and Mike Wallace completed the top five. Sentimental favorite Harry Gant, driving his last Winston Cup race, could manage only 33rd place, but left the tour with his popularity at the same high level he established early in his career.

Hovering over his fleet, Bob Bondurant brings 35 years of top-level motorsports experience to his School of High Performance Driving, now in its 27th year of operation. A win at LeMans (1964) with Dan Gurney in a Ford Cobra Daytona coupe, the World Manufacturers' Champion with Carroll Shelby and Ford the following year, plus a stint as a Ferrari Formula One driver are the highlights in his personal driver's log book. He now presides over a school fleet of 150 specially prepared Ford and Lincoln-Mercury vehicles, a team of top notch instructors, and a state-of-the-art facility at Phoenix's Firebird International Raceway. Bondurant School graduates include such celebrities as Paul Newman, Tom Cruise, Clint Eastwood, Candice Bergen, and Crystal Bernard, as well as professional racing drivers Al Unser Jr. the '94 IndyCar champion, Dale Earnhardt the '94 Winston Cup champion, Bill Elliott, Rick Mears, and Mark Martin.

DRIVERS

Scott Pruett shows speed and maturity
in taking the Trans-Am title.

The economy being what it is, lots of Americans work more than one job. One of the more successful two paycheck practitioners, IndyCar driver Scott Pruett, took some weekends off (13 to be exact) from his first job, testing for the Firestone equipped and sponsored Pat Patrick IndyCar team prior to its return to competition in '95 and added the hotly contested '94 Trans-Am Tour driver's title to his resume. Pruett exhibited both a high turn of speed and maturity of judgement in capturing the title in the Goodyear-shod Royal Oak Camaro. Had Tommy Kendall, expected to be the top performer of a trio of very serious and very swift Ford drivers and his crew taken a slightly more conservative approach, he might well have escaped the penalties that relegated him to third place in the championship. Kendall won more races than Pruett (four to three) but paid heavily for a driving infraction and two technical violations that could be attributed to his All Sport backed team. Kendall gained the opening honors in Miami and was quickly countered by a Pruett win at Mosport. Kendall initiated the real fireworks at Mid-Ohio, tagging leader Ron Fellows on the last lap, spinning him out. Kendall took the lead and the victory. Winner Kendall called the nudge a "racing incident". The officials viewed it differently, penalized him 16 points. Pruett assumed the top spot in the championship chase and kept it through the end-of-season Dallas event. Not, however, without some help from Kendall's crew. At Road America, Kendall placed second on the track but was disqualified for an illegal fuel cell. The cell wasn't too big, but the safety oriented "flapper" was missing. His points and prize money were forfeited, effectively ending his season long pursuit of Pruett for the title. Perhaps feeling they had nothing to lose, Kendall's crew was nabbed in the final Dallas round for changing tire compounds on a pit stop. Kendall's third place points and prize money went the way of those sacrificed at Road America. Pruett's crew could hardly point fingers; they were charged with using illegally grooved rain tires at the Glen, a violation the SCCA officials rated as a 10 point demotion.

None of the above detracts from Pruett's title, earned by a clear focus on the task at hand. He was out qualified only by Kendall (seven poles to four), completed every lap, had 10 podium appearances. Trans-Am cars are notoriously tough on tires, so that tire strategy can often determine a close race's outcome. Pruett's long hours of testing for Firestone, albeit in a different vehicle, gave him a valuable background of experience. He put it to good use, particularly in earning his second place behind Ron Fellows in Detroit. A matched pair of second places at Portland and Des Moines, coupled with a sparkling

wire-to-wire win at Cleveland, earned him a slight bulge in the points, negated by a mechanical gremlin that dropped him to 10th at Trois Rivieres. Pruett repeated his Cleveland performance, leading every lap from the pole, at Road Atlanta, to again build a useful cushion in the Trans-Am Tour points chase. Pruett's only regret, in a banner year, was that the always exciting, hotly contested Trans-Am Tour didn't have a sponsor, an item SCCA Pro Racing's top two, Dan Greenwood and Kevin O'Brien, are assiduously pursuing for 1995 and beyond. One long time observer National Speed Sport News' Bill Oursler called Trans-Am, "Racing's best kept secret." It's no secret among the series' fans that the nose-to-tail, paint scraping, two and three abreast style of Trans-Am front runners provides excellent value for the money. It doesn't hurt that the two biggest domestic nameplates, Ford and Chevrolet, are the principal protagonists, and that the racing machinery has a reasonable resemblance to their showroom products.

For Kendall, '94 was a "coulda been" year. Despite topping the statistics, except in the all important points category, he maintained that he was out to win races and let the points take care of themselves. They did, his 276 points were good enough only to tie for third in the championship. To add to his leadership in races won, (four, a tie with Ron Fellows) and poles, (seven) he led the most miles (419) and the most laps (234).

Canadian Ron Fellows, like Kendall, Mustang mounted, qualified as the hard luck "king" of the Tour, managed to finish second in the title chase despite his misfortunes. They started early in the season at Mid-Ohio, the third round. Fellows led every lap, from polesitter Kendall, except the last one when he was nudged from the rear by Kendall who went on to win. A game Fellows salvaged ninth place.

Determined to regain momentum, Fellows came back to win the next two, Detroit and Portland, the latter from the pole, leading every lap. After a third at Des Moines, the gallant Canadian produced, at Cleveland, perhaps his finest performance. An innocent victim of a king sized first lap crash not of his doing, he displayed true tenacity to earn third place from far back in the field. The bad luck in hometown Toronto was of his own making, a spin in an over ambitious attempt to get by a slower car. While the weather at Watkins Glen was rainy, a trip to the winner's circle at Watkins Glen provided sunshine for Fellows, this after a stop-and-go penalty at the start. A freak accident at Road Atlanta dropped him to the bottom area of the finishing chart. A competitor's crashed car, tagged by Pruett, launched a solid piece of debris in his direction, scoring a direct hit on a vital part of his

car's anatomy. This unhappy incident took him out of the championship. Spirit undampened, he won the Dallas season finale, auguring well for the '95 season.

Tying Kendall in the points chase at 276, Dorsey Schroeder often showed the on-track form that earned him the '89 Trans-Am title. He was the only driver other than the top three to score a victory. His two wins against Kendall's four dropped him to fourth place in the season's standings. The first of these, at Des Moines, involved both good luck and fortitude. A hot, dehydrated Schroeder nursed a failing gearbox home in front, after leader Kendall ran out of fuel. The second, at Road America, involved a wild, last lap restart in which Schroeder prevailed in a shoot out with Pruett and Fellows, punctuated by shredding fiberglass. Schroeder posted fastest lap of the race on six occasions, a measure of his prowess on the circuit. Schroeder could easily contest Fellows' "back luck king of '94" title. A blown tire at Mosport impacted his car's bodywork, dropped him to 19th at the end. At Portland, Cleveland, and Dallas, accidents not of his making knocked him out of the top ten.

Paul Gentilozzi, returning to the circuit full time, was the top "non-factory" Chevrolet driver. No wins, but a season high second place in the Dallas finale gave him momentum for '95, adding to his fifth place standing in the '94 points chase. Regular front runner Jack Baldwin endured a disappointing season, marked by mechanical failures, posted seventh place in the season's standings. A strong second place at Cleveland was his best outing. Bobby Archer switched to a Mustang for '94, placed third in the Dallas finale, seventh in the points standings.

Greg Pickett, in the colorful Rain-X Cytomax Camaro, posted eight top 10 finishes, good for eighth place in the season's standings. His bright yellow Chevrolet was regularly a favorite with the crowd. He'll be back in '95 for another try at the crown vacated by Scott Pruett. Tim McAdam and Tommy Archer, like his brother Mustang mounted, rounded out the top 10.

While all of the top half dozen drivers of '94, except champion Pruett, are expected back in '95, they can look for some spirited competition from the graduating '94 rookie crop, the deepest and most talented in a decade. The Nimrod Press Rookie of the Year award went to Tim McAdam, who finished every race in the top 20, six in the top 10. He nipped Jamie Galles, son of IndyCar racing team owner Rick Galles, for the honor. Other standout rookies include Boris Said and Brian Simo, who split the driving duties of a Gloy Racing Mustang. Even with standout Pruett gone, it won't be any easier to take the Trans-Am Tour driver's title in '95.

Steve Mohlenkamp

1. Worthy winner...**Scott Pruett** exhibited speed, consistency and *intelligence*. His second Trans-Am drivers' title, well earned, is a solid springboard for his return to the IndyCar wars.

2. Lacking only luck...**Ron Fellows** tied for most race wins (4), scored two poles, two fastest race laps. Only one of the several incidents that cost him heavily were of his making.

3. Penalties hurt...**Tommy Kendall** posted seven poles and four wins, proof that he is fast. Crew miscues and resultant penalties shattered his title hopes.

4. Longer races needed…**Dorsey Schroeder** had six fastest race laps and two wins to demonstrate his talent. Regularly "ran out of laps" with fastest car on the circuit, late in the race.

5. Proven front runner...**Paul Gentilozzi** scored no wins, one fastest race lap, but showed that he can run with the top performers. Runner up spot at season end Dallas round augurs well for '95.

6. Tough year…**Jack Baldwin** suffered a rash of mechanical failures which took their toll in a season that was expected to be better.

7. Successful switch…**Bobby Archer** joined the Ford forces and scored one fastest race lap. His season end podium placement in Dallas should be an omen for improved '95 season.

Steve Mohlenkamp

8. Consistent veteran...**Greg Pickett** notched five top five placements in his Rain-X/Cytomax Camaro, confirmed his skills and consistency.

Steve Mohlenkamp

9. Auspicious debut…**Tim McAdam,** the top rookie of '94, rolled to seven top 10 placements, which indicate a move up in his sophomore '95 year.

10. Brother act…**Tommy Archer** placed in the top five three times to earn a solid top 10 season standing. He too switched to Ford.

11.

One race short...**Jamie Galles** made the podium in his first race of the year. Unfortunately, it was the second race on the schedule, or he might have been Rookie of the Year.

12.

Dallas standout...**Ray Kong** saved his best effort for the last race of his rookie season, breaking into the top five in Dallas.

13.

One bad break…**Jon Gooding** will long remember the handsome fifth place in Dallas that went flying when he lost his brakes, triggered a four car pile up.

Steve Mohlenkamp

Steve Mohlenkamp

14.

Outstanding rookie…**Boris Said** had heads turning in his debut year. Unfortunately, it ended midseason when he had to turn his car over to Brian Simo.

15.

Two top 10s…**R.J. Valentine** had a midfield season highlighted by two top 10 finishes.

16.

Another outstanding rookie…**Brian Simo** and Boris Said made an outstanding rookie team. Only hitch, they shared the same car. Their combined point total would have topped the rookie ranks.

Steve Mohlenkamp

17.

Two top 10s…**Bruce Barkelew** had a season somewhat similar to R.J. Valentine's, also posted two top 10 finishes.

18.

One top 10…**Bill Saunders** made the elite top 10 category once, in Toronto.

19.

Just missed a top 10…**Philip Bartelt** twice came close to a top 10 finish.

Steve Mohlenkamp

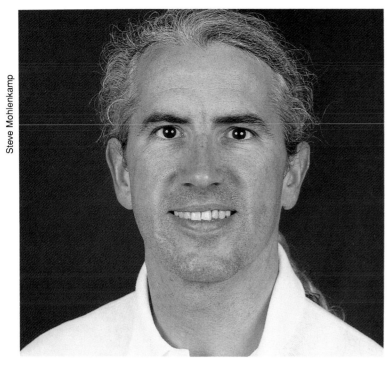

Steve Mohlenkamp

20.

Missed three races…**Ric McCormick** sat out three '94 events or his two top 10 results would have earned him a higher placement.

1994 TRANS-AM TOUR
DRIVERS' CHAMPIONSHIP POINT STANDINGS

POS	DRIVER/CAR	POINTS	PURSE	MI	MS	MO	DT	PO	DM	CL	TO	TR	WG	AT	RA	DA
				\multicolumn{13}{FINISHING POSITION}												
1	SCOTT PRUETT, Camaro	341	$123,550	3	1	2	2	2	2	1	2	10	5	1	2	4
2	RON FELLOWS, Mustang	307	174,025	5	4	9	1	1	3	3	13	5	1	20	3	1
3	TOM KENDALL, Mustang	276	182,350	1	2	1	3	3	6	19	1	1	3	3	31	24
4	DORSEY SCHROEDER, Mustang	276	135,600	2	19	4	7	12	1	18	3	2	2	2	1	18
5	PAUL GENTILOZZI, Camaro	271	94,738	6	6	3	6	7	5	5	4	8	4	13	6	2
6	JACK BALDWIN, Camaro	212	67,450	4	11	14	13	4	18	2	6	3	23	4	17	15
7	BOBBY ARCHER, Mustang	202	61,450	8	7	6	29	9	4	9	18	7	8	15	19	3
8	GREG PICKETT, Camaro	196	62,149	–	5	5	5	8	8	7	17	4	16	23	4	16
9	TIM McADAM*, Camaro	187	37,500	14	13	15	14	11	10	10	8	19	9	7	13	8
10	TOMMY ARCHER, Mustang	177	49,300	7	12	8	30	6	16	4	5	6	26	22	5	19
11	JAMIE GALLES*, Camaro	166	44,460	–	3	27	4	15	13	6	16	17	17	6	10	9
12	RAY KONG*, Camaro	155	35,200	16	25	12	21	14	19	8	10	11	14	17	11	5
13	JON GOODING, Mustang	134	40,300	19	9	28	31	10	22	12	7	13	7	16	20	17
14	BORIS SAID*, Mustang	128	24,600	10	10	7	8	5	7	–	–	–	–	–	7	–
15	R.J. VALENTINE, Camaro	120	32,650	32	17	26	10	16	20	17	12	18	13	11	25	7
16	BRIAN SIMO*, Mustang	119	22,475	–	–	–	–	20	–	11	19	9	10	5	9	6
17	BRUCE BARKELEW, Camaro	100	24,800	22	–	23	23	17	12	21	14	15	19	10	26	10
18	BILL SAUNDERS, Mustang	98	26,950	13	24	34	16	13	21	13	9	16	12	25	30	24
19	PHILIP BARTELT, Mustang	87	19,800	–	–	20	19	–	15	15	–	–	11	14	16	11
20	RIC McCORMICK*, Camaro	78	15,600	11	21	10	22	25	–	–	–	20	20	19	8	26
21	BOB PATCH, Trans Am	65	11,700	21	22	16	27	27	–	23	–	–	21	9	15	13
22	RANDY RUHLMAN, Dodge	63	18,700	33	14	21	25	–	11	14	–	12	–	26	–	22
23	DONALD SAK, Cutlass	50	13,200	–	16	25	24	–	–	20	11	–	15	21	29	–
24	ROBBIE BUHL*, Mustang	38	5,200	–	–	11	12	21	–	22	–	–	–	–	–	–
25	DALE PHELON, Camaro	33	5,100	28	18	29	17	–	–	–	–	–	24	24	14	–
26	DARIN BRASSFIELD, Camaro	30	4,200	–	–	13	9	–	–	–	–	–	–	–	–	–
27	DEBORAH GREGG, Mustang	29	4,000	–	–	–	15	–	–	–	–	–	–	8	–	–
28	BRIAN RICHARDS, Camaro	28	3,200	–	15	17	–	18	–	–	–	–	–	–	–	–
29	R. K. SMITH, Camaro	24	4,200	9	–	–	–	–	–	–	–	–	–	–	24	21
30	MIKE BERG*, Mustang	24	3,400	29	–	–	18	24	–	–	–	–	–	–	–	12
31	RICK DITTMAN, Cutlass	24	3,200	–	20	–	–	–	–	–	–	–	–	12	22	–
32	IRV HOERR, Camaro	23	2,900	17	–	33	–	–	–	–	–	–	–	–	12	–
33	CRAIG SHAFER, Camaro	22	2,600	–	–	22	–	–	–	16	–	–	18	–	31	–
34	BILL GRAY, Camaro	21	2,800	–	–	36	11	–	–	–	–	–	–	–	–	20
35	ROBERT RIZZO, Mustang	20	3,600	–	–	–	–	–	–	–	–	–	6	–	27	–
36	GEORGE ROBINSON, Camaro	18	2,700	31	8	–	–	–	–	–	–	–	–	–	–	–
37	CLINT WELDING, Camaro	18	2,500	–	23	–	–	–	–	–	15	–	22	–	–	–
38	JIM DERHAAG, Camaro	17	2,500	–	–	–	–	–	9	–	–	–	–	–	28	–
39	MITCH BENDER, Camaro	16	1,800	–	–	18	–	–	–	–	–	–	–	–	18	–
40	ERIC WELLS, Camaro	15	2,100	27	–	–	28	23	–	–	–	–	–	–	–	14

MI: Miami **MS:** Mosport **MO:** Mid-Ohio **DT:** Detroit
PO: Portland **DS:** Des Moines **CL:** Cleveland **TO:** Toronto
TR: Trois-Rivieres **WG:** Watkins Glen **AT:** Road Atlanta **RA:** Road America
DA: Dallas *1994 Trans-Am Nimrod Press Rookie of the Year Candidate

A TALE OF TWO CAMAROS

Savvy sponsor Dave Ohlhausen backed two front running Camaros in the '94 Trans-Am Tour, rookie Jamie Galles whose white Entrepreneur/Rain-X coupe is shown putting the pressure on veteran Gregg Pickett in the Rain-X/Cytomax car. Galles notched third place at Mosport, the only rookie to gain a podium position all year. 1989 champion Pickett picked up five top five placements.

TRANS-AM TOUR MANUFACTURERS CHAMPIONSHIP FALLS TO FORD

FORD: 10 firsts, 2 seconds, 3 thirds, 109 points
CHEVROLET: 3 firsts, 7 seconds, 2 thirds, 90 points

Steve Mohlenkamp

Ford forces, led by the Mustang mounted trio of Ron Fellows, Tom Kendall, and Dorsey Schroeder, with an assist from Bobby Archer, outgunned Chevrolet, the '93 titleholder, in the Manufacturers Championship. Camaro driver Scott Pruett, who notched the drivers championship, was aided and abetted by Red Bowtie devotees Paul Gentilozzi and Jack Baldwin in the manufacturers competition. The Ford quartet combined for 10 wins, 9 poles, 9 fastest race laps, and led 70% of the race laps.

Trans-Am Tour
Round 1
Miami Street Course
February 27, 1994

Tommy Kendall in Mustang starts fast, finishes first, in Miami season opener.

The top trio of Ford Mustang Cobra drivers, Tommy Kendall, Dorsey Schroeder, and Ron Fellows served notice at the opening round of the '94 Trans-Am Tour that they will be tough to beat. Kendall notched the pole, edged a fast closing Schroeder at the wire by .434 seconds. Also serving notice were Camaro teammates, Scott Pruett and Jack Baldwin, who shouldered Fellows aside to take the third and fourth slots at the end. If any team can master the Ford group, Pruett and Baldwin are the likeliest. The top four Miami finishers are former champions eyeing a second title in 1994. The race, in itself, was a coup for the Tour since it was the first time that Trans-Am was the feature event on the Miami circuit. Kendall picked up a single race Trans-Am record purse of $22,500 as well as the Flowmaster Star of the Race designation. Schroeder impressed the fans with his charge through the upper half of the field, which fell just short of victory but earned him the fastest lap honors. Boris Said, a second generation driver, made the race's top 10 and went to the head of the class in the competition for Rookie of the Year honors.

Trans-Am Tour
Round 2
Mosport Park
May 22, 1994

Scott Pruett and Chevrolet take Mosport on the rebound.

Camaro driver Scott Pruett evened the score in his personal tug o' war with Ford protagonist Tommy Kendall on the scenic Mosport circuit, winning with a comfortable 12.68 seconds in hand. To be sure, Kendall, the Miami first round winner was again on the pole, albeit only a tick quicker than second qualifier Pruett. In a sense, both Pruett and Kendall were lucky. Pruett inherited the lead early when Kendall went from first to fourth on a miscue. Kendall got his second place as a gift from then second place Jack Baldwin whose engine blew up on the last lap, spilling oil on the circuit. Among the victims of the spill, rookie Boris Said, having a great run until his oil-induced trip into the tire barriers. Among the beneficiaries, Kendall and rookie Jamie Galles, who scored a third place in the Entrepreneur/Rain-X Camaro in his first outing of the year. Fourth place Ron Fellows was sandwiched in between Galles and the Rain-X/Cytomax Camaro wheeled by Greg Pickett, who picked up fifth place. Not a bad day for sponsor Dave Ohlhausen. With the Ford and Chevrolet forces now engaged in earnest, trackside observers could detect little difference resulting from minor bodywork adjustments required by the SCCA after the opening race. These presumably took away a bit from the Mustangs, gave a tad to the Camaros. At this early point in the proceedings, it's an even-money bet.

Trans-Am Tour
Round 3
Mid-Ohio, Lexington, OH
June 5, 1994

Tommy Kendall and Ford go one up with Mid-Ohio victory.

At Mid-Ohio, for the third time in the season's three Trans-Am Tour races of '94, Tommy Kendall garnered the pole in his Mustang. For the second time, he was also in the top spot at the end. This one was no clear cut wire-to-wire romp, like the Miami opening round. Fellow Ford driver Ron Fellows outdragged Kendall at the start, led every one of the race's 45 laps, except the all-important last one. A late race incident brought out the yellow, and Fellows might easily have won the race under caution. It was not to be. The green came out with only a single lap left. Fellows and Kendall squirted away from third place Scott Pruett and fourth place Paul Gentilozzi. Fellows prevailed through the first two corners. On the third, Kendall, sensing a passing opportunity, "went for it", tapped Fellows just hard enough to send him gyrating into the infield. Result; Kendall wins, Chevrolet standard bearers Pruett and Gentilozzi follow him across the finish line. SCCA officials called Kendall's pass "unsafe", docked him $6000 and 16 points. Pruett became the Tour's point leader. Fellows called it, "Disappointing. We should have won." Not disappointed was Greg Pickett who piled up his second top five finish in a row, just behind fourth place Dorsey Schroeder.

Trans-Am Tour
Round 4
Belle Isle Park, Detroit, MI
June 11, 1994

Ron Fellows and Ford take top honors in the Motor City 100.

This is the Trans-Am race they all turn out for, the occupants of glass walled corner offices, computer oriented engineers, assembly line workers and just plain car enthusiasts. It's all in the name; the Motor City 100, a Chevrolet/Ford confrontation in which the winning nameplate automatically gets hometown bragging rights for a year. Overcoming his Mid-Ohio disappointment, Ron Fellows took the pole, lost the lead to Scott Pruett on lap two, reclaimed the top spot for good with six laps to go. No less than three full-course yellows were displayed in response to accidents on the beautiful, but difficult to pass circuit. The last of these, on lap 38 of the 48 scheduled, afforded Fellows his passing shot at Pruett. Tires, as usual at Detroit, wore out fast. Fellows noted, "I had a little more rear grip at the end. When I was clear, I was gone." His 12.59 second margin of victory bears out his statement. Pruett's fading tires held up well enough for second place. Tommy Kendall's bet on a two tire yellow flag pit stop fell short. He ended up third. Rookie Jamie Galles and veteran Greg Pickett, both Rain-X backed, notched fourth and fifth. There was even a multi-car crash after the checker waved for Fellows. Boris Said, the promising rookie, and Detroit's own Robbie Buhl were the principal victims. In its first year as the event's organizer, IMG's Motorsports Marketing Group turned out a record crowd for the weekend.

Steve Mohlenkamp

Trans-Am Tour
Round 5
Portland International Raceway, Portland, OR
June 25, 1994

Ron Fellows makes it two in a row at Portland.

Polesitter Ron Fellows drove a near perfect flag-to-flag race for his second Trans-Am win in a row at Portland's colorful street circuit. The victory matched Fellows' 1993 Portland win. Though only 1.91 seconds ahead of third qualifier Scott Pruett at the end, Fellows was never seriously threatened. Second fastest qualifier Tommy Kendall shadowed Fellows for the first 21 laps before sliding off course and letting Pruett by. Kendall's misadventure cost him only one place as he rejoined the circuit in the third slot and held it to the end. "It was nice to be in the lead right away," admitted a happy Fellows in victory circle. Pruett gave full marks to the winner. "I was just trying to keep up with Ron. I couldn't catch him." Kendall attributed his miscue to a fumbled downshift. "I was lucky to get out of it with no damage." Jack Baldwin took fourth place despite front bodywork that was shaking. Hard driving rookie Boris Said had no bad luck this time, cracked the top five. Winner Fellows moved into a tie with Kendall for second place in the Tour championship at 128 points, 12 astern of leader Pruett with 140. Ford now leads Chevrolet, 43 to 35, in the Manufacturers Championship.

Steve Mohlenkamp

Trans-Am Tour
Round 6
Des Moines Street Circuit
July 4, 1994

Dorsey Schroeder tops the charts at Des Moines.

Better luck, better strategy, or both propelled Dorsey Schroeder into the lead over polesitting, front running Tommy Kendall with two laps remaining on the Des Moines street circuit. Kendall, who had led from the start, ran out of fuel with the victory seemingly in hand. True, as Schroeder, the Raybestos Mustang driver, said, "I was running at Tommy real hard, I think I was forcing him to run harder," which could have been a factor in Kendall's fuel consumption. Equally true, Schroeder had little chance of catching Kendall except for his miscalculation. Other beneficiaries of the Kendall miscue were second finishing Scott Pruett and third place Ron Fellows. Pruett maintained, "We knew coming in, that this track would be tough on tires, brakes, and transmissions. We have to conserve the car." A modest Fellows stated, "We just had to survive. We didn't have the speed to catch the top three." To add to Kendall's woes, when he did get his car to crawl to the pits to refuel, he was penalized for his crew's failure to wear correct refueling suits. Kendall's misadventure cost him his second place in the championship points. At 151, he was passed by Fellows with 153. Pruett with 167, remains on top. Ford continues to lead the manufacturer's competition over Chevrolet, 52 to 42.

Trans-Am Tour
Round 7
Burke Lakefront Airport, Cleveland, OH
July 9, 1994

Scott Pruett and Chevrolet are back on top at Cleveland.

Tiring of the runner up role he's played for the last four races, Scott Pruett earned star billing for himself and his Royal Oak Charcoal Camaro on Cleveland's fast Burke Lakefront Airport circuit. Pruett impressed a banner Trans-Am crowd with his wire-to-wire dash to victory circle. Fastest in qualifying, Pruett allowed no other driver even a look at first place. Pruett's crew overcame a blown clutch in the morning practice session, had his Camaro back in prime condition for the green flag. Pruett's teammate Jack Baldwin avoided the bad luck that has dogged him this season, finished second for a Camaro 1-2. Pruett credited his testing program for the Firestone-tired Pat Patrick IndyCar team he'll drive for in '95, with a strong assist. "Testing with Firestone has taught me to conserve tires and be consistent. Both items will help us to win the championship." Robbie Buhl made Pruett's task easier by triggering a multi-car accident that took out the top four Fords on the first turn of the first lap. Buhl manfully admitted his mistake, "I saw an opening. I thought I could get by. The car went sideways and onto the grass. On the grass you're just along for the ride." Ron Fellows, in an heroic ride, recovered from the first lap tangle to finish third after being down to 19th place. Tommy Archer and Paul Gentilozzi rounded out the top five.

Trans-Am Tour
Round 8
Toronto Street Circuit
July 16, 1994

Tommy Kendall is tops in Toronto.

Recovering from the first lap Cleveland accident in which he was an innocent victim, Tommy Kendall displayed his pole and race winning form in Toronto's Raybestos Trans-Am Classic. It wasn't easy. Fellow Mustang driver Ron Fellows, in front of a wildly partisan hometown crowd, displaced Kendall for the lead on lap 14. Basking in cheers from the stands, Fellows stayed in front until he overreached in passing a back marker on lap 43. His miscue let Kendall back into the lead, now ardently pursued by Scott Pruett, who fell short by a mere .20 seconds, and Dorsey Schroeder. Pruett admitted he couldn't challenge Kendall at the beginning. "I just held my own pace, let the race settle down and things came together." Schroeder had a good run, complained only of too few laps. "I had a lot of race car at the end. We just ran out of laps." Paul Gentilozzi notched fourth place, followed across the line by Tommy Archer. Fellows had to deal with a damaged clutch when he tried to restart after his spin, limped home in 13th place. With his fifth second place of the season, "Mr. Consistency" Scott Pruett enhanced his lead in the driver's championship, 227 points to Fellows' 192. Kendall's win upped his total to 191, within striking distance of second place.

Trans-Am Tour
Round 9
Trois-Rivieres, Canada
August 7, 1994

Tommy Kendall makes it two in a row at Trois-Rivieres.

Tommy Kendall won the Trois-Rivieres Grand Prix "his way", out in front, flag-to-flag, from the pole position. The flying Mustang driver had a comfortable .76 seconds cushion over Dorsey Schroeder at the end, to post his second victory in a row, his fourth for the year. Despite the lack of a serious challenge on the track, Kendall called it, "Good, hard racing. We took a chance on a new set up after qualifying. Fortunately the car ran very well in the race." Schroeder, moving up smartly from his fifth place starting position while posting fastest race lap, repeated his Toronto lament, "We just ran out of laps." "Mr. Consistency", Scott Pruett, uncharacteristically failed to make a podium appearance for the first time this year. He did salvage a top 10 finish, while nursing a failing rear axle seal the entire second half of the race. Jack Baldwin took down third place as Ron Fellows faded to fifth. Greg Pickett drove the bright yellow Rain-X/ Cytomax Camaro to a strong fourth place. Kendall's win bounced him back into second place in the drivers championship, where he trails Pruett, 243 to 224. Fellows was demoted to third place at 213 points.

Trans-Am Tour
Round 10
Watkins Glen, NY
August 3, 1994

Ron Fellows masters a wet Watkins Glen.

Ron Fellows stood tall at the top of an all Ford winner's podium at a wet Watkins Glen. Considering the handicaps the courageous Canadian faced and overcame, he was justified in the open delight he displayed in victory. For openers, his engine misfired on the first pace lap, so he dashed into the pits. His crew's emergency ministrations seemed to help. He noted, "Whatever they did, it cleared up a lot." Understandably anxious, Fellows jumped the start after rejoining the track at the rear of the field. The SCCA officials then jumped on Fellows, sent him back to the pits again for a stop-and-go penalty. Once firmly in the race, Fellows wasted no time in making up for lost ground. After 10 laps he was in sixth place, then out dueled Paul Gentilozzi for fifth. On a lap 22 restart, he made a spectacular end run around the top four to gain the lead. Fellows noted, "Getting by Gentilozzi was the tough part. On the restart the motor cleared up completely and we were on our way." "On our way" ended up as a comfortable 9.6 second margin over second place finisher Dorsey Schroeder. Third finisher Tommy Kendall was in the lead when he was passed by Fellows and Schroeder at the same place on the circuit. Gentilozzi ended up in fourth place. Scott Pruett earned the pole but finished fifth. His crew cost him 10 points and $3000 in prize money for using prohibited hand grooved tires. Pruett's lead over Kendall in the title chase shrank to four (255 to 251) with Fellows in contention at 244.

Trans-Am Tour
Round 11
Road Atlanta
August 27, 1994

Scott Pruett bests Dorsey Schroeder and Tom Kendall in Blockbuster Trans-Am.

Arriving at Road Atlanta's challenging road circuit with only a four point lead over Tommy Kendall in the driver's championship, Scott Pruett left with a 12 point advantage after winning the Blockbuster Trans-Am. The win was a typical Pruett clutch performance. He captured the pole, turned in a near perfect winning performance. Not that Kendall didn't try. He pushed Pruett hard in the early stages before deciding that further aggression would induce too much tire wear and be counter productive. Ron Fellows, very much in the title chase, was disappointed by his fourth place qualifying effort, made some amends by passing third qualifier Dorsey Schroeder at the start. Fellows chances went glimmering when he collected debris from a Bill Saunders/Dale Phelon collision that leaders Pruett and Kendall escaped without damage. Unlucky Fellows ended up in 20th position. Hard running Dorsey Schroeder got by Kendall, no mean trick on the Road Atlanta circuit, but could make no impression on Pruett. This time he voiced no implication that he could have made the pass except for running out of laps. He admitted that Pruett could come off the corners better and get away. Jack Baldwin finished fourth after a penalty for passing under the yellow. Fifth place went to rookie Brian Simo, a notable achievement.

Trans-Am Tour
Round 12
Road America, Elkhart Lake, WI
September 10, 1994

Dorsey Schroeder takes the Texaco-Havoline 200 in a virtuoso performance.

It's a true road circuit, fast and smooth and Dorsey Schroeder loves it. Road America's Texaco-Havoline 200 provided the perfect venue for his smooth, come-from-behind driving style as the Mustang pilot notched his second victory of the year. Moving up swiftly from his sixth starting position, Schroeder collared polesitter and first half leader Scott Pruett just past the halfway mark, passed him cleanly. Schroeder's margin of victory at the end was a clear cut 2.40 seconds. Schroeder's trip to the top was eased by a Tommy Kendall miscue in a passing attempt on Pruett. Kendall, who finished third on the track, suffered further misfortune when a post race inspection found his fuel cell to be without its mandatory flapper, a safety device required to limit fuel spill in the case of an accident. The penalty; loss of all race points and prize money. Pruett and Ron Fellows engaged in an all out drag race to the finish line, Pruett got the edge by inches. Greg Pickett in the Rain-X/Cytomax Camaro notched fourth place ahead of Tommy Archer.

With one race remaining Pruett has locked up the Trans-Am Drivers Championship with 318 points, followed by Kendall with 276 and Fellows with 275. Ford has already notched the Manufacturers Title.

Trans-Am Tour
Round 13
Dallas, TX
September 18, 1994

Ron Fellows first in the Ford Grand Prix of Dallas.

Taking his cue from the event's title, Ford mounted Ron Fellows ended the '94 Trans-Am season in Dallas on a winning note. The victory capped a year of 10 wins in 13 races for Ford, gaining for the blue oval the Manufacturers Championship won by Chevrolet's red bowtie forces in '93. Polesitter Tommy Kendall led for only a single lap, giving way to second qualifier Paul Gentilozzi's Camaro for the next 22 laps. Fellows was handed the lead when Gentilozzi spun in an attempt to put a lap on Randy Ruhlman. Gentilozzi recovered quickly but felt that the spin took the edge off his car. "I took a chance, damaged the front of the car, and it developed a real push." Not enough of a push to keep him out of second place, however. On lap 50, Jon Gooding, running in fifth place, lost his brakes, plowed into fourth place Greg Pickett in the Rain-X/Cytomax Camaro. Pickett's car ended up on Jack Baldwin's Camaro. Pruett took a slight hit in the wild proceedings but was able to continue. Gooding, Pickett, and Baldwin were not so fortunate. Tommy Kendall had race long tire problems, still finished third, but faced his second disqualification in a row for changing tire compounds on a pit stop. Bobby Archer finished third. New champion Pruett was fourth and rookie Ray Kong placed fifth. IMG's fast growing Motorsports Group is expected to take over organization of the Dallas Grand Prix in '95.

Geoffrey Hewitt

Exxon Supreme GTS Championship
Nissan driver Steve Millen back on top

Gallant Steve Millen, coming back from the heartstopping midseason '93 crash that took him out of contention for that year's Exxon Supreme GTS Driver's Championship, regained the title he last held in '92. Millen started the season in high style as a key member of Clayton Cunningham's Nissan 300 SX team that won the Rolex 24 at Daytona outright, the first ever GT (production car based) team to humble the top line WSC cars of '94 or their GTP (prototype) predecessors. It was no fluke. Millen and the Cunningham team did it again at Sebring's 12 hour endurance run, with a different set of driver teammates which included Irishman Johnny O'Connell, who ended up second in the Driver's Championship. For the third round, at Road Atlanta, the WSC and GTS contingents ran separately, as they would for the balance of the schedule, which afforded no further chance to embarrass the theoretically faster category. Since Road Atlanta was the site of the Ferrari 330SP debut, chances were slim that the production based Nissan 300 SX team could have prevailed, particularly in a sprint race. Millen did prevail in the

separate GTS race, however, bringing his Nissan home on top of the charts, for three in a row.

By round four, the New England Dodge Dealers Grand Prix at Lime Rock, Irv Hoerr had a different Detroit nameplate humming, his Rain-X Oldsmobile Cutlass Supreme from the Brix Racing stable. Hoerr won the race, as he would the next two rounds, for three in a row. Even in winning, Hoerr couldn't keep Millen off the podium, as the Nissan driver piled up useful points even in defeat. Indeed, Millen never finished outside the top three for the entire season. By round seven, at Laguna Seca, the Nissan forces had found new legs, and captured the victory. It wasn't Millen in the top spot, however, but teammate O'Connell. For round eight, at Portland, the Nissan pendulum swung back to Millen. Back again to O'Connell went top honors at the season ending Phoenix round. Millen's second place at Phoenix sealed the Driver's Championship for him, with O'Connell ranking second in the season's points and Oldsmobile's Rain-X backed Irv Hoerr, third on the basis of his exceptional

three race victory string in midseason. Nissan's 175 points garnered the 1994 GTS Manufacturer's title over Oldsmobile with 140. Millen was a big contributor.

A Nissan driver also took down top honors in the GTU category for production based GT cars of 2.0 to 3.8 liter displacement. Leitzinger Racing's Jim Pace won three races in his Nissan 240 SX. At Portland, Butch Hamlet added another Nissan win. Eduardos Dibos and Bill Auberlen, Mazda mounted, combined for three victories. The GTU honors in the season opening endurance races went to Porsche 911 RSRs. For the year, Pace, Dibos, and Auberlen were the top three drivers. In the "stand alone" races following the two endurance contests, competition at the top was spirited and spectator enthusiasm was high.

In the separate GTO category, which started its season in Atlanta, Mustang driver Joe Pezza earned the driver's title on the basis of four single victories in the seven events. Olds driver Brian DeVries posted a single win, was the runner up.

DRIVERS

IMSA launches World Sports Car Championship
Wayne Taylor takes the first Exxon WSC drivers title

Braver in a business sense, than most of the drivers his group sanctions are on the track, new owner Charles Slater became the IMSA CEO just before the '94 opening round, the Rolex 24 at Daytona. "A lot of people thought I was crazy," admits Slater. Not without justification. The new World Sports Car Championship, replacing the immensely popular, manufacturer backed GTP (for prototype) series, was unproven. Even IMSA's schedule of races was infirm. The principal sponsor, R.J. Reynolds, had bowed out at the end of '93. Ten months later it appeared that Slater had beaten the odds. The World Sports Car (WSC) category, boosted by the introduction of four high revving, fast moving, 12 cylinder Ferrari 333SP spyders, with all the tradition and crowd appeal attached to the Maranello marque, proved popular. A nine race schedule was solidified, and corporate heavyweight Exxon, already involved in another IMSA series, for GT cars, picked up the World Sports Car series sponsorship. Certainly IMSA's task in '95 will be easier.

Now that there was a WSC series, who won it? Not one of the Ferrari drivers as might be expected. The champion turned out to be Wayne Taylor, driver of Jim Downing's Mazda Kudzu. Downing himself finished third in the series, based on points earned sharing Taylor's car and those obtained in his other Kudzu, this one with Buick power. Downing is not only a competent driver but a total gentleman. At season's end he switched driving assignments on his team around to help Taylor land the title, when he could have won it himself. Downing's self-sacrificing actions marked him as a true sport in a sport that becomes more businesslike with every passing season. Ferrari didn't win the manufacturer's title either. Oldsmobile did, by dint of the efforts of talented Canadian driver Jeremy Dale and his team owner, Harry Brix. Brix provided the financial backing to campaign and develop the Brix Olds Spice that got better and better as the season progressed. Dale and his Olds powered hybrid won outright in the Portland round and sealed the manufacturers championship with pole position and race win at Phoenix. You didn't know that Olds powered a front line IMSA

World Sports Car racer? Neither did a lot of other people who follow motorsports. To correct this oversight, Olds ran a very telling ad in enthusiast publications. It pictured two identical world globes, one titled: "The world before we beat Ferrari.", the other: "The world after we beat Ferrari." and noted that while it hadn't changed the world much, a $330,000 Oldsmobile had beaten the pants off some million dollar Ferraris. Olds powered Dale earned the runner up spot in the Driver's Championship.

Generous Jim Downing placed third in the Driver's Championship aboard his Kudzus, ahead of fourth place Andy Evans, the top Ferrari point gainer. Bob Schader, who organized the Olds Spice effort, placed fifth in a Buick Kudzu, after stepping down as the Olds Spice co-driver to give Dale a cleaner shot at the title. Eliseo Salazar was the second best placed Ferrari driver. He garnered sixth place in the season's point totals. In seventh place were a colorful pair, British driver James Weaver and the bright yellow Rain-X Ferrari Spice of sportsman Rob Dyson. This car's engine was not a built-for-racing V12 of the $1 million 333SPs but a hotted up version of the production V8 found in garden variety $125,000 348 Ferraris. Regularly the crowd favorite, Weaver delighted in tweaking the front runners, but the car rarely exhibited the stamina to be a factor at the end. Fermin Velez was third on the list of Ferrari 333SP drivers, eighth in the overall standings. Paul Debban in a Buick Kudzu, and Hugh Fuller, Chevrolet Spice, completed the top 10.

Since Kudzu chassis were the vehicle of choice for half of the top 10 drivers in the Exxon WSC Championship, one might speculate that the name is derived from some swift and exotic form of antelope. It's not. Kudzu is a rugged Asian vine used widely for erosion control. In '94 its namesake chassis eroded a lot of high hopes in other quarters.

How did transplanted-to-Florida South African David Taylor, perfectly cast for his role as David, humble the Ferrari Goliaths (the drivers of all four cars)? First, the Ferraris not yet up to endurance tasks, wisely elected to skip Daytona's daunting Rolex 24 and Sebring's 12 Hour marathon, made their first appear-

ance at Atlanta. Without winning a race, Taylor simply "out pointed" everybody else, including Dale who did win two races outright. Though not in contention for the overall win in the first two events, where top honors went to Nissan GTS production based cars, Taylor and Downing drove the second place WSC car at Daytona and Sebring, affording them a point lead that lasted all year, and generated Taylor's championship and Downing's third place in the standings. Taylor's third place in the season finale at Phoenix, coupled with Downing's generosity, sealed the title. In between, solid but not spectacular finishes and a reliability record that included only one DNF piled up the points. None of this should take any lustre from Taylor's performance. He drove hard and intelligently, extracted the maximum points possible from his admittedly underpowered car. As a measure of his ability, he was hired by the MOMO Ferrari team to drive in the '95 Rolex 24 at Daytona, along with the ex-Formula One pilot Eliseo Salazar and ex-IndyCar chauffeur Didier Theys.

When the Ferraris *did* arrive, at Road Atlanta, they arrived in a hurry. Jay Cochrane set the pace in the Euromotorsport entry with a winning 116.04 mph average speed, a full lap ahead of the rest of the field. For the next three rounds it was the MOMO team of Gianpiero Moretti and Eliseo Salazar front and center on the winners' podium as the top Ferrari entry. For round seven at Laguna Seca, Fermin Velez and Andy Evans of the Scandia entry got their turn at being the head of the Ferrari class. To the surprise of the crowds at Portland and Phoenix, the steady improvement of the Brix team upended the Ferrari contingent and landed driver Dale in the winner's circle. Dale did it from the pole in the final Phoenix round. He lapped the entire field in a virtuoso performance that fell just short of unseating Wayne Taylor, the points leader going into the race. While the Ferraris failed to capture the Manufacturers Championship, they did win five races outright and the hearts of fans long starved for the competition appearance of the Italian thoroughbreds.

Kudzu Cousins…"Gentleman Jim" Downing shared his Mazda Kudzu with Wayne Taylor, gave Taylor the preferred late season seat that led to Taylor's WSC Driver's Championship. "Good Guy" Downing still finished third in the WSC Driver's points.

David Outpoints Goliath...**Wayne Taylor**, though a non-winner, extracted more points from his Mazda Kudzu than seemed possible, more than any other driver in the series.

Ferrari Fighter…**Jeremy Dale** challenged all year, gained sufficient momentum to win last two races overall.

Eric Wunrow

Dual Role…**Bob Schader** organized the successful Brix Olds Spice effort for Dale, as well as driving his own Buick Kudzu.

Three Time Winner…**Eliseo Salazar** came out of retirement to drive **Gianpiero Moretti**'s Ferrari 333SP to three victories in a row. Moretti "fathered" the 333SP concept.

Fast Britisher…**James Weaver** was part of the winning WSC team at Sebring on loan from his regular Dyson Ferrari ride. In Dyson's Rain-X Ferrari he regularly harassed the leaders. He's shown with **Geoff Brabham.**

Ferrari Driver...**Fermin Velez** shared a 333SP and one victory with car owner Andy Evans.

Nissan Kingpin…**Steve Millen** was the mainstay of Nissan 300SX driving teams that won Daytona and Sebring overall, captured two solo GTS events for the series title. Teammate Johnny O'Connell partnered Millen at Sebring, won two solo events to make it close.

Olds Standout…**Irv Hoerr** hustled his Rain-X Olds to three solo GTS victories in a row, battled the Nissan forces all the way to the Phoenix finale.

Geoffrey Hewitt

Geoffrey Hewitt

First Ferrari Victor…**Jay Cochran** wasn't supposed to win for Ferrari in the debut of the much heralded 333SPs but he did, harrying Ferrari test driver Mauro Baldi along the way.

Ferrari Factory Man…**Mauro Baldi**, factory test pilot for the Ferrari 333SPs, had his pole winning car flying in the Atlanta opener, was grounded by a failed suspension.

MORETTI

SALAZAR

CRISTAL

EXXON

30
MOMO
GOODYEAR

CRISTAL®

AGLIETTO

NISSAN 300ZX GTS takes top honors
bests new World Sports Cars in Rolex 24 At Daytona

After qualifying and before the start of the '94 Rolex 24 At Daytona, the odds makers picked a production based GTS car, Nissan or Porsche, to win the 32nd running of the endurance classic. The experts opined that the new World Sports Cars debuting here had little chance of carrying their speed twice around the clock. As odds makers so often are, they were right. Paul Gentilozzi, IndyCar driver Scott Pruett, Butch Leitzinger, and Steve Millen drove one of Clayton Cunningham's well proven pair of Nissan 300ZXs into the victory circle with 24 laps to spare over the second place car. This, too, was a GTS runner, the Porsche 911 Turbo with an international driving team headed by Bob Wollek, a multiple winner here, and Juergen Barth. Not even the experts predicted that the first of the presumably faster WSC cars to finish would punch the clock back in ninth place. This was the Olds Spice with a driving team headed by Jeremy Dale and Price Cobb, which had qualified second. The pole winning Chevrolet Spice with Andy Evans and IndyCar driver Ross Bentley on the team was a casualty, completing only 223 laps. As a testimony to durability, four Porsche 911 RSRs competing in the lower rung GTU class occupied finishing positions 3-4-6-8, delighting their holiday minded privateer drivers, all from outside the U.S., and a cheering Porsche spectator contingent.

A well prepared Olds Cutlass, with Irv Hoerr, Tommy Riggins, and Price Cobb on the driving team finished a commendable fifth (and, at sixth fastest, didn't qualify too badly either). An almost box-stock Chevrolet Corvette backed by Mobil, with Andy Pilgrim and Stu Hayner as half of the driving team, placed seventh. The second best WSC car, a Mazda Kudzu with lead drivers Wayne Taylor and Jim Downing, its owner, rounded out the top 10. Spectator turnout was excellent, despite the disappointment inherent in Ferrari's decision not to unleash their sleek 333SP WSC cars until IMSA's third round at Atlanta.

Rolex Watch USA President and CEO Roland Puton presents the winners award to the star-studded driving team of Scott Pruett, Paul Gentilozzi, Butch Leitzinger and Steve Millen as well as a personal Rolex to each.

Scott Pruett of the winning Nissan team handicapped the race quite accurately before the start. "We're running a strong, proven car. I came here for the overall win and the car we'll have to beat is the Brumos Porsche." The Brumos Porsche 911 Turbo would indeed be a threat, until it shredded a fan belt, affecting both the turbo and the bodywork and was eventually withdrawn, a severe disappointment to its all star driving team of Hans Stuck, Walter Rohrl, IndyCar driver Danny Sullivan, and the winningest Daytona 24 Hour driver, Hurley Haywood. Second finisher Bob Wollek, a frequent occupant of victory circle here, took little solace in the runner up spot earned by his Porsche 911 Turbo team. "It's an achievement. At the same time it's the worst thing in the world." Gunter Doebler was ecstatic over the record shattering (for the GTU category) run of his third place overall Porsche 911 RSR team. "The

A pair of Mobil backed almost stock Corvettes performed well, one earned a worthy seventh place overall.

greatest victory we've ever had. And it's our first time here. We're just weekend racers." Mark Sandridge was only slightly less happy about his Porsche 911 RSR team's fourth place on the chart. "We had a great battle (with Doebler's class winning Porsche), we had fun, and it was a *real* race." The fifth place Olds Cutlass could have been in contention for top honors, except for two mishaps; an afternoon "agricultural" excursion that bent the undertray and a lost input shaft, which took the best part of an hour

to replace. Driver Tommy Riggins rightly acclaimed the team's spirit. "When you've finished this race you've accomplished something."

Rob Dyson stated his position on his new WSC car accurately. "Blazing trails has its drawbacks. This was only a test session for us." Or as Jeremy Dale said of his ninth place WSC category winning Olds Spice. "Our car is only in its sixth week of development. We're going to get much better." By season end he had turned out to be a man of his word.

The Motorola Olds Spice won World Sports Car honors for its ninth place overall finish in Daytona's inaugural event for IMSA's new open cockpit class.

Geoffrey Hewitt

NISSAN 300ZX
makes it two in a row at Contac 12 Hours of Sebring

After the runaway Nissan 300ZX win in the Rolex 24 At Daytona, IMSA lowered the boom on the high flying GTS front runners. That is they lowered the Nissan's allowable boost pressure by a full eight inches. This move made it a closer contest with the new for '94 WSC contingent, but couldn't keep one of Clayton Cunningham's immaculately prepared Nissans out of the overall winner's circle in the second of the season's endurance events, the Contac 12 Hours of Sebring. Steve Millen was again the lead driver on the winning team (Cunningham saved him for the critical final driving stint). This time his teammates were transplanted Irishman Johnny O'Connell and John Morton. The top WSC car, the Spice/Chevrolet driven by car dealer (Auto Toy Store)/car owner Morris Shirazi and a top British trio, Derek Bell, Andy Wallace, and James Weaver (on a weekend off from his Rob Dyson Rain-X Ferrari ride) made it a lot closer, only five laps down. Wayne Taylor and Tim McAdam, along with car owner Jim Downing, posted a well earned third overall aboard their Mazda Kudzu. This

despite a spate of oil cooler problems that necessitated two unscheduled pit stops. Andy Evans and Butch Leitzinger, aided by IndyCar driver Ross Bentley, driving a Chevrolet Spice, nailed down fourth place overall.

This reversal in World Sports Car fortunes, while short of the overall win, can be translated two ways. The WSC contingent learned a lot at Daytona and applied it. 12 hours is a lot shorter than 24. With the first two endurance classics over and the series moving to much shorter, separate races for the all out WSC cars and the production based GTS group, there will be no immediate opportunity to compare them head-to-head. It is notable, however, that in the last third of the race Millen & Co. added an additional three laps to their lead. Mark Sandridge's fifth place overall (with co-drivers Joe Varde and Nick Ham) gained him and his Porsche 911 RSR the top GTU spot. Butch Hamlet, Jim Pace, and Barry Waddell were six laps astern in the Nissan 240 SX for second place GTU honors and sixth overall. Three Porsches, a 911 Turbo

and two 911 RSRs occupied the next three places at the end. An unusual entry, the Chevrolet engined Consulier, with Scott Lagasse and Winston Cup front runner Ken Schrader at the helm, rounded out the top 10. Hurley Haywood experienced a second disappointing endurance outing in a Porsche 911 Turbo, just missed the top 10 despite the efforts of top line co-drivers Hans Stuck and Walter Rohrl. Once again mechanical gremlins moved him down the chart.

From here it's on to Road Atlanta where the fabled Ferrari 333SPs are scheduled to debut. Unless the pure-bred Ferraris prove fragile, the hybrid WSC cars which contested the two early season endurance races will have to make further progress over their considerable Sebring gains to stay competitive. In GTs, can anyone else catch the front running Nissans? Not if Rod Millen has anything to say about it. "This car is just so strong and so reliable. It's a fantastic start to the season."

Geoffrey Hewitt

FERRARIS START FAST
finish 1-2 in their WSC debut at Road Atlanta

The Ferraris have landed and are taking no prisoners. The long delayed and much anticipated debut of the Ferrari 333SP WSC cars came off at Road Atlanta on schedule and almost according to the script. As expected, the thoroughbred V12s took the first two places. Since there is always a twist in any Italian drama, the winner was not, as expected, polesitter and factory test driver Mauro Baldi but privateer/owner Jay Cochran, considered the least likely of the four Ferraris entered to prevail. Baldi did his job, running smoothly at the front for the first two-thirds of the race, albeit not getting away from Cochran. On lap 65, Cochran passed Baldi, seemingly without effort. Baldi's Ferrari had let him down with what proved to be a terminal case of suspension failure. Now the Ferrari fortunes were in Cochran's hands— and in second place was the ATS Chevrolet Spice driven by Andy Wallace. Could this opening act turn tragic? Not to worry. No mourning in Maranello. Bounding out from the wings in a fast recovery from an earlier spin, came Eliseo Salazar in a third Ferrari. He stalked and handily passed Wallace to place Ferraris 1-2 in their World Sports Car debut to the delight of a large spectator assemblage, gathered to witness just that result. Wallace held on to third place at the end, just ahead of the Wayne Taylor/Jim Downing Mazda Kudzu. IndyCar driver Ross Bentley co-drove the fourth Ferrari entered with owner Andy Evans to fifth. Jeremy Dale, who drove the Olds Spice with the second fastest qualifying time, another surprise to Ferrari forces, could have been a spoiler, but his car succumbed to mechanical woes. Verdict on the Ferrari debut; fast, as expected, perhaps a little fragile, not totally unexpected. It certainly was not the Maranello runaway in the script, but then those beautiful V12, 4 cam, 5 valve per cylinder engines are running at IMSA imposed rev limits, substantially short of the power output of which they're capable.

In the separate GT race, Steve Millen continued his winning ways in the Cochran Nissan 300 ZX, first overall, first in GTS. Joe Pezza, Mustang mounted notched the GTO win. Jim Pace earned double honors for Nissan, taking the GTU win in his 240SX.

LIME ROCK falls to Ferraris, 1-2-3
Moretti and Salazar on top

Second time out the Ferrari forces did what their fans expected of the sleek V12 333SPs, nail down all three places on the victory podium. Top billing went to the pair of Eliseo Salazar and Gianpiero Moretti in the MOMO car that Salazar put on the pole. The win was particularly gratifying to 54 year old Moretti, a long term IMSA driver and supporter as well as the prime mover in convincing Ferrari to build the 333SPs. Jay Cochran, winner at Atlanta in the 333SPs' debut picked up second spot, while Andy Evans and Charles Morgan completed the Ferrari hat trick. The proceedings were enlivened at the drop of the green flag when James Weaver in the other variety of Ferrari, the bright yellow Rain-X machine with a mere 8 cylinders, darted in front and held off all attempts by Salazar, an ex-Formula One driver, and Mauro Baldi, the Ferrari test driver, to dislodge him. He even conned Salazar into a failed passing attempt that let third place Baldi get by. This crowd pleasing

game was over on lap 34 as Baldi finally asserted the might of his 12 cylinder technology. Not long after Weaver was out with brake problems. Baldi didn't last much longer, giving in to suspension problems. What about the big American engined cars? Not their day. The only one to poke a nose in front, and that only for five laps, was Price Cobb in the Olds Spice, who with driving partner Rich Sutherland, finished fifth, behind the reliable Mazda Kudzu of Wayne Taylor and Jim Downing and ahead of the Jeremy Dale/Bob Schader Olds Spice. Will the rest of the WSC season be a Ferrari festival? Could be, but the Olds contingent is far from giving up. The nagging question of WSC sponsor was answered when a happy Charles Slater, the IMSA Chairman, announced a three year pact with Exxon.

In the separate GT race, controversy reigned in the paddock and fiberglass was shredded on the track. When the acrimony simmered

down, two Olds Cutlasses were on top, breaking the stranglehold that the Cunningham Nissan 300ZX had placed on the series in the person of three-time winner Steve Millen. Not only did the Cutlasses, both Rain-X backed and driven by Irv Hoerr and Darin Brassfield, win, they claimed the front row in qualifying. The first item of contention was the Nissan's boost pressure, which Brix Racing, the Olds entrant, contended was over that allowable. IMSA agreed and fined the Nissan team. The Nissan camp claimed that Brassfield punted Millen, who was trying to complete a last lap pass, into the tire wall. IMSA ruled the incident to be one of the non-punishable "racing" variety. (Neither driver lost a place). Joe Pezza and his Mustang topped the GTO category in fifth place overall. Mazda mounted Bill Auberlen, won the GTU division in sixth place overall. Overall a spectacular event, one in which the Lime Rock spectators enjoyed some very close competition.

Steve Mohlenkamp

James Weaver in the 8 cylinder Rain-X Ferrari Spice frustrated the V12 333SP contingent, leading the first 34 laps.

Olds pacesetter Irv Hoerr took the pole and the GTS race win, nudging the Nissans out of the spotlight.

Dan Bianchi

Geoffrey Hewitt

FERRARI makes it three in a row at the Glen
Salazar and Moretti repeat

The Glen Continental, at three hours duration, seemed to be just the right ticket for a second Ferrari sweep, not too long, not too short. As things turned out, only one of the three Ferraris entered (The fourth failed to show up, reportedly enmeshed in financial problems.) was running at the end, unchallenged in first place. Eliseo Salazar and Gianpiero Moretti had upheld Maranello's honor again. Up until five laps from the end that honor had been in jeopardy. The other 333SPs were sidelined, Mauro Baldi and Jay Cochran's car with engine problems after only 15 laps, Andy Evans', with IndyCar pilot Eddie Cheever co-driving, with an engine fire after 58. Second place Jeremy Dale in the Olds Spice, who led on two occasions earlier, was carving huge chunks out of Moretti's lead and was only five seconds behind on lap 75. That's where the Dale charge ended, undone by a suspension failure that almost sent Dale into the Armco. James Weaver,

in the Rain-X Ferrari Spice, again made it interesting in the early stages, actually leading the race for nine laps. With owner Dyson at the wheel for the last driving stint, the car developed gearbox problems and faded to ninth overall at the finish. While the WSC contingent was fading fast, the lead GTS cars were just as swiftly moving up the ladder, despite some deterrents handed them by IMSA. First, all GTS cars had their fuel capacity lowered to 18 gallons from the 26 allowed them previously. That translated to four pit stops instead of three. Next the Nissan 300ZX runners had four pounds of boost slashed from their allowable turbocharger pressure. As the unhappy Nissan drivers predicted, both of the Brix Olds outqualified the single Cunningham Nissan entered. Irv Hoerr's Lime Rock winning Olds proved the fastest of the Brix pair, finishing second overall, and on the same lap as the winning Ferrari. The Millen/O'Connell Nissan, down two

laps at the finish in third place overall, did manage to beat the second Olds wheeled by Darin Brassfield, with the help of some tire changing miscues by Brassfield's crew. Hurley Haywood's Le Mans class Porsche 911 Turbo, co-driven by Hans Struck, finally had a trouble free outing, landing him in fifth place overall and clinching, for Porsche, the North American GT Endurance Championship. Brian de Vries' GTO category Olds Cutlass notched sixth place overall and first in class. Charles Morgan's Camaro, also a GTO runner, was next across the finish line. Though not running at the end, the Jeremy Dale/Bob Schader Olds Spice had piled up enough laps for the seventh place overall. Peruvian Eduardo Dibos shrugged off a spin in his Mazda to claim first in GTU. The Watkins Glen round demonstrated the vulnerability of the WSC cars when asked to run more than sprint distances.

THREE IN A ROW
for the Salazar/Moretti duo at Indianapolis Raceway Park

Eliseo Salazar handed over the leading 333SP to owner Gianpiero Moretti with a comfortable 40 second cushion and less than 10 laps to go in IMSA's inaugural Indianapolis Raceway Park outing. It almost wasn't enough. A hard charging Fermin Velez in his first Ferrari drive, this aboard Andy Evans' 333SP, came close to nailing Moretti at the wire. Only intervening traffic saved the third win in a row for Moretti, while co-driver Salazar sweated out the finish in the pits. James Weaver made it an all Ferrari podium, sneaking his Rain-X backed, V8 engined hybrid into third place after the two V12 thoroughbreds. Jeremy Dale gave the Ferrari camp serious cause for concern, qualifying his Olds Spice on pole and leading the first six laps. His potential late race charge fizzled

when Dale's throttle jammed open, requiring an unwanted extra pit stop. It didn't help that Dale's seat belts had come loose, just prior to this delay. Circulating steadily, if unspectacularly, all day was the faithful Mazda Kudzu of Wayne Taylor and Jim Downing. No fireworks, but a fifth place finish, matching Taylor's qualifying position and sufficient points to maintain the lead in the drivers' championship.

A wild shoot-out between the Nissan and Olds forces in the separate Exxon Supreme GT sprint saw Irv Hoerr's Rain-X Olds come out on top. Not without a little help from his polesitting teammate, Darin Brassfield who took out Nissan driver Johnny O'Connell as he was applying pressure to leader Hoerr with three laps to go. Hoerr inherited the

lead from Nissan mounted Steve Millen who spun while avoiding a back marker with six laps left. The net result: Hoerr first, Millen second, O'Connell third, and Brassfield fourth. IMSA later penalized Brassfield, taking away his points and prize money. While there was little love lost between the Nissan and Olds camps pre-race, their post-race relationship reached a new low. Joe Pezza's Mustang picked up GTO honors. Eduardo Dibas, Mazda mounted, had the GTU category wrapped up until a late race caution gave Jim Pace the opportunity to position his Nissan 240SX to better advantage in the ensuing traffic, which he did. The race was less than 100 miles long but endowed with more heated encounters than many of twice the length.

Steve Mohlenkamp

FIVE IN A ROW FOR FERRARI
Fermin Velez and Andy Evans take top honors at Laguna Seca

Geoffrey Hewitt

Ferrari confirmed its domination of IMSA's Exxon World Sports Car series by taking its fifth race in a row at Laguna Seca. No other marque has made it to victory circle since the thoroughbred V12 333SPs arrived on the scene at Atlanta. Fermin Velez, in co-driver Andy Evans' 333SP, passed leader Eliseo Salazar with only a handful of laps remaining in the two hour sprint to notch the victory. Salazar was enjoying a 30 second lead, but needed a splash-and-go fuel stop for his 333SP to make it to the finish. A race spin by points leader Wayne Taylor in the Mazda Kudzu dropped him to eighth place and gave Salazar the opportunity for a quick fuel stop without sacrificing the lead. What he did sacrifice was the chance to take

on fresh tires. Velez's better shod 333SP quickly overtook Salazar. Jeremy Dale in the Motorola Olds Spice claimed third place. The third Ferrari entered, driven by Jay Cochran and Russell Spence was fourth. James Weaver in the Rain-X Ferrari Spice, who diced with the leaders in the early going, was fifth, a lap behind, at the end. Andy Wallace in an Olds Spice out qualified the entire Ferrari contingent and led handily until being slowed and finally sidelined by engine problems.

The Laguna Seca round of the WSC series was notable in that leaders appear to be coming closer to each other and the Olds powered Spices now represent a serious threat to the Maranello contingent. With two events yet to come can

Ferraris sweep all seven events in which they were entered? The Olds camp, unintimidated, takes a firm negative view of this possibility.

The separate one hour Exxon Supreme GT event started, and ended, as a Nissan 300ZX benefit. Johnny O'Connell, Steve Millen and Eric Van de Poele qualified in that order and finished the same way. Irv Hoerr and Darin Brassfield, the Olds GTS standard bearers had to be content with fourth and fifth places. GTO points leader, Mustang mounted Joe Pezza added to his edge with another win. Jim Pace, leading the GTU runners in his Nissan 240SX, also added to his points cushion with a win, coming from behind to nip Mazda mounted Eduardo Dibos and Bill Auberlen.

JEREMY DALE in his Olds Spice
beats the Ferraris—and the rain in Portland

Portland's next to last WSC round was an up and down affair. What went up was the airborne Olds Spice driven by Hugh Fuller whose miscue launched him atop the Ferrari 333SP driven by Fermin Velez. Fuller and the Spice survived the encounter, which was climaxed by Fuller righting his half overturned vehicle and motoring on to an eventual fifth place finish. Velez's Ferrari, half of the Maranello contingent in the race, did not. Understandably Velez and the Ferrari's co-driver Andy Evans were less than amused. What came down was the rain, hard enough to stop the race for 25 minutes and stop it for good after racing resumed. The other 333SP, the Salazar/Moretti entry suffered bad luck of a different sort, a time consuming spin by owner Moretti early in the contest, which co-driver Salazar could not overcome.

These mishaps smoothed the path of second fastest qualifier Jeremy Dale in the Motorola Olds Spice into the lead, which he held when the race was called. Salazar's strenuous efforts earned his team the runner up position. The surprise third place driver was Jim Downing in his own Buick Kudzu co-driven by Ferdinand Di Lesseps. Fourth place went to the Comferdam/Mandeville Mazda Hawk. Downing, in a generous strategy move, allowed points leader, friend Wayne Taylor to take Taylor's Mazda Kudzu out solo on a points hunting mission. This mission failed badly when Taylor was rear ended on the first lap by Bob Schader in the second Olds Spice. It took more than 10 laps to get the Kudzu back on the course and the best finish Taylor could eke out was ninth. Taylor's comfortable cushion in the points chase was washed away in Portland's rain. It would take the final Phoenix round to decide the championship and Dale's car is faster. In the separate GT contest Steve Millen put his Nissan 300ZX's superior handling in the wet to good advantage and brought off the GTS win for the second Nissan victory in a row. Tommy Riggins in his Olds Cutlass put a dent in Joe Pezza's GTO points lead by taking top category honors. Butch Hamlet in his 240SX made it a GT double for Nissan by taking down GTU honors.

Steve Mohlenkamp

Steve Mohlenkamp

JEREMY DALE wins Phoenix finale
Wayne Taylor takes the drivers title

Jeremy Dale and his Brix Racing Team did all they could, put their Olds Spice on the pole and in the winner's circle, beating all three Ferrari 333SPs at Phoenix International's season finale, a two hour after dark sprint. But they couldn't keep Wayne Taylor off the podium. Third place in his reliable Mazda Kudzu earned Taylor IMSA's first ever Exxon World Sports Car Drivers Championship. Consolation prize for the Brix group was the Manufacturers Championship their Phoenix victory handed to Oldsmobile. Both titles, Drivers and Manufacturers, had been undecided going into the final round. Jay Cochran had the fastest of the three 333SPs in qualifying, ahead of Andy Evans, James Dyson in the 8 cylinder Ferrari Spice, and Gianpiero Moretti in the third 333SP.

Dale out jumped the opposition at the start and in typical fashion Weaver harried the two 333SPs ahead of him, getting smoothly past Evans. Dale and Cochran opened a gap, one that Evans would further open when he got past Dale after

10 laps. Weaver and Eliseo Salazar, replacing Moretti, then tangled after a lap 39 restart. The collision moved both back in the field. Far enough back that leader Cochran with Dale in tow became involved in an all Ferrari tangle as he attempted to lap Salazar. Cochran's 333SP was severely damaged, handling impaired. Salazar escaped unharmed but was now two laps down to the flying Dale in the lead. Wayne Taylor and Jim Downing did not repeat their Portland miscue. They let other drivers start both Kudzus and Taylor hopped into the leading one on the first pit stop and started a relentless move up the charts. Fermin Velez in Andy Evans' 333SP, mounted a stern challenge to Dale at this juncture, was tripped up by a freak mishap; his lights wouldn't work. Rather than face the inevitable black flag, Velez came in for repairs, which turned out to be anything but quick and dropped him to sixth place at the end.

The net result, Dale first, Salazar and Moretti second. The title clinching third place went to Wayne Taylor.

The Hugh Fuller/Andy Wallace Chevrolet Spice and the James Weaver/John Paul Jr. Ferrari completed the top five. Cochran was disconsolate that he hadn't been able to secure the manufacturer's title for Ferrari, after seemingly having had the race in hand. But not being ready for the season's first two events might have been even more crucial to Ferrari's failed first attempt at the title.

In the separate Exxon Supreme GT event, the Nissan forces took no chances, entered three of the potent 300ZX machines. The strategy worked, Nissans finished 1-2-3. Johnny O'Connell was top man, followed by Steve Millen, and Belgian Eric Van de Poele. Millen's second place secured for him the GTS driver's title. In GTO, Joe Pezza, the Mustang proponent, had already won the title. Paul Gentilozzi and Camaro took the race win. In GTU, Mazda man Bill Auberlen posted the win but Jim Pace, a Nissan 240SX exponent, notched fourth place and the division championship.

The Mazda Kudzu that could, and did, carry Wayne Taylor to the first ever Exxon World Sports Car Drivers Championship.

Geoffrey Hewitt

1994 IMSA SEASON POINT STANDINGS

MANUFACTURERS POINT STANDINGS

Exxon WSC	Exxon Supreme GTS	Exxon Supreme GTU
Oldsmobile **163**	Nissan **175**	Nissan **139**
Ferrari **159**	Oldsmobile **140**	Porsche **129**
Mazda **158**	Porsche **70**	Mazda **124**
Buick **137**	Chevrolet **49**	Lotus **12**
Chevrolet **136**		

DRIVERS POINT STANDINGS

Exxon WSC	Exxon Supreme GTS	Exxon Supreme GTU
1. Wayne Taylor **190**	1. Steve Millen **137**	1. Jim Pace **105**
2. Jeremy Dale **187**	2. Johnny O'Connell **129**	2. Eduardo Dibos **101**
3. Jim Downing **178**	3. Irv Hoerr **117**	3. John O'Steen **88**
4. Andy Evans **168**	4. Darin Brassfield **85**	4. Bill Auberlen **76**
5. Bob Schader **160**	5. Eric Van de Poele **34**	5. Mark Sandridge **71**
6. Eliseo Salazar **158**	6. Paul Gentilozzi **28**	6. Butch Hamlett **63**
7. James Weaver **119**	6. Scott Pruett **28**	7. Joe Cogbill **53**
8. Gianpiero Moretti **107**	6. Jeff Pattinson **28**	3. Joe Varde **40**
9. Paul Debban **103**	6. Bruce Trenery **28**	9. Jack Lewis **38**
10. Fermin Velez **95**	10. Hurley Haywood **27**	10. Joachim Rohr **36**
	10. Hans Stuck **27**	

TOYOTA PRO/CELEBRITY RACE

One of the spectator highlights of the motorsports year is the Toyota Pro/Celebrity Race contested on the same Long Beach circuit over which the IndyCar drivers battle for gold and glory in the Toyota Grand Prix of Long Beach. Mounted on equal safety prepared, but otherwise stock, Toyota Celicas, the professionals strive mightily to overcome each other and the celebrities, who get the benefit of a handicapped start. Overall winner of the '94 event was Alfonso Ribeiro of *The Fresh Prince of Bel-Air*, who edged out professional Brian Redman. Sean Astin of *Rudy*, Anthony Smith of the Los Angeles Raiders, and David Alan Grier of *In Living Color* provided spirited competition in the celebrity ranks. Shinji Sakai, President and CEO of Toyota Motor Sales U.S.A., Inc., made the presentations in victory circle.